THREAD

:he photographed items were made using ›edspread weight cotton thread (size 10). Any of he following brands may be used with good esults:

\unt Lydia's® Classic Crochet
Coats Opera 10
DMC® Baroque
DMC® Cebelia
DMC® Cordonnet Special
DMC® Traditions
Grandma's Best
. & P. Coats® Knit-Cro-Sheen®
South Maid®
Lily® Antique

WASH

For a mo
washed a
warm wa
wring, ge
Rinse several times in cool, clear water. Roll piece in a clean terry towel and gently press out the excess moisture. Lay piece on a flat surface and shape to proper size; where needed, pin in place using rust-proof pins. Allow to dry **completely**.

CROCHET TERMINOLOGY	
UNITED STATES	**INTERNATIONAL**
slip stitch (slip st)	= single crochet (sc)
single crochet (sc)	= double crochet (dc)
half double crochet (hdc)	= half treble crochet (htr)
double crochet (dc)	= treble crochet (tr)
treble crochet (tr)	= double treble crochet (dtr)
double treble crochet (dtr)	= triple treble crochet (ttr)
skip	= miss

STEEL CROCHET HOOKS															
U.S.	00	0	1	2	3	4	5	6	7	8	9	10	11	12	13	14
Metric - mm	3.5	3.25	2.75	2.25	2.1	2	1.9	1.8	1.65	1.5	1.4	1.3	1.1	1	.85	.75

BEGINNER	Projects for first-time crocheters using basic stitches. Minimal shaping.
EASY	Projects using yarn with basic stitches, repetitive stitch patterns, simple color changes, and simple shaping and finishing.
INTERMEDIATE	Projects using a variety of techniques, such as basic lace patterns or color patterns, mid-level shaping and finishing.
EXPERIENCED	Projects with intricate stitch patterns, techniques and dimension, such as non-repeating patterns, multi-color techniques, fine threads, small hooks, detailed shaping and refined finishing.

We have made every effort to ensure that these instructions are accurate and complete. We cannot, however, be responsible for human error, typographical mistakes, or variations in individual work.

Production Team: Instructional Editor - Susan Ackerman Carter; Technical Editor - Linda Luder; Lead Graphic Artist - Rachel Burgess; Graphic Artist - Rebecca J. Hester; Photo Stylist - Janna B. Laughlin; and Photographer - Russ Ganser.

Doilies made and instructions tested by Belinda Baxter, Marianna Crowder, Freda Gillham, and Mary Valen.

Excellent

Stitch Guide

FRONT POST SINGLE CROCHET
(abbreviated FPsc)
Insert hook from **front** to **back** around post of st indicated ***(Fig. 2, page 1)***, YO and pull up a loop, YO and draw through both loops on hook.

FRONT POST DOUBLE CROCHET
(abbreviated FPdc)
YO, insert hook from **front** to **back** around post of sc indicated ***(Fig. 2, page 1)***, YO and pull up a loop (3 loops on hook), (YO and draw through 2 loops on hook) twice.

FRONT POST TREBLE CROCHET
(abbreviated FPtr)
YO twice, insert hook from **front** to **back** around post of dc indicated ***(Fig. 2, page 1)***, YO and pull up a loop (4 loops on hook), (YO and draw through 2 loops on hook) 3 times.

FRONT POST CLUSTER
(abbreviated FP Cluster) (uses next 5 sts)
YO twice, † insert hook from **front** to **back** around post of **next** FPtr ***(Fig. 2, page 1)***, YO and pull up a loop, (YO and draw through 2 loops on hook) twice †, YO twice, skip next dc, insert hook from **front** to **back** around post of next FPdc, YO and pull up a loop, (YO and draw through 2 loops on hook) twice (3 loops remaining on hook), YO twice, skip next dc, repeat from † to † once, YO and draw through all 4 loops on hook.

SPLIT FRONT POST TREBLE CROCHET
(abbreviated Split FPtr)
First Leg: YO twice, insert hook from **front** to **back** around post of st indicated ***(Fig. 2, page 1)***, YO and pull up a loop, (YO and draw through 2 loops on hook) twice (2 loops remaining on hook).
Second Leg: YO twice, insert hook from **front** to **back** around post of st indicated, YO and pull up a loop, (YO and draw through 2 loops on hook) twice, YO and draw through all 3 loops on hook.

Instructions continued on page 5.

DOILY

Ch 6; join with slip st to form a ring.

Rnd 1 (Right side)**:** Ch 3 **(counts as first dc, now and throughout)**, dc in ring, ch 1, (2 dc in ring, ch 1) 7 times; join with slip st to first dc: 16 dc and 8 ch-1 sps.

Rnd 2: (Slip st, ch 1, sc) in next dc, ch 2, 3 dc in next ch-1 sp, ch 2, skip next dc, ★ sc in next dc, ch 2, 3 dc in next ch-1 sp, ch 2, skip next dc; repeat from ★ around; join with slip st to first sc: 32 sts and 16 ch-2 sps.

Rnd 3: (Slip st, ch 1, sc) in first ch-2 sp, skip next dc, work FPsc around next dc, sc in next ch-2 sp, ch 3, ★ sc in next ch-2 sp, skip next dc, work FPsc around next dc, sc in next ch-2 sp, ch 3; repeat from ★ around; join with slip st to first sc: 24 sts and 8 ch-3 sps.

Rnd 4: Ch 1, sc in same st, ch 3, skip next FPsc, sc in next sc, 5 dc in next ch-3 sp, ★ sc in next sc, ch 3, skip next FPsc, sc in next sc, 5 dc in next ch-3 sp; repeat from ★ around; join with slip st to first sc: 56 sts and 8 ch-3 sps.

Rnd 5: (Slip st, ch 1, sc, ch 3, sc) in first ch-3 sp, skip next sc, work FPsc around next dc, (ch 2, work FPsc around next dc) 4 times, ★ (sc, ch 3, sc) in next ch-3 sp, skip next sc, work FPsc around next dc, (ch 2, work FPsc around next dc) 4 times; repeat from ★ around; join with slip st to first sc: 56 sts and 40 sps.

Rnd 6: (Slip st, ch 3, 2 dc, ch 3, 3 dc) in first ch-3 sp, ch 3, working **behind** ch-2 sps, sc in center dc of next 5-dc group on Rnd 4, ch 3, ★ (3 dc, ch 3) twice in next ch-3 sp on Rnd 5, working **behind** ch-2 sps, sc in center dc of next 5-dc group on Rnd 4, ch 3; repeat from ★ around; join with slip st to first dc: 48 dc and 24 ch-3 sps.

Rnd 7: Ch 3, ★ † work FPtr around next dc, dc in next dc, 7 dc in next ch-3 sp, dc in next dc, work FPtr around next dc, dc in next dc, work FPdc around next sc †, dc in next dc; repeat from ★ 6 times **more**, then repeat from † to † once; join with slip st to first dc: 112 sts.

Rnd 8: Working in Back Loops Only ***(Fig. 1, page 1)***, slip st in next 2 sts, ch 4, dc in next dc, (ch 1, dc in next dc) 7 times, work FP Cluster, ★ dc in next dc, (ch 1, dc in next dc) 8 times, work FP Cluster; repeat from ★ around; join with slip st to third ch of beginning ch-4: 80 sts and 64 ch-1 sps.

Rnd 9: (Slip st, ch 1, sc) in first ch-1 sp, (ch 3, sc in next ch-1 sp) 7 times, ★ ch 1, sc in next ch-1 sp, (ch 3, sc in next ch-1 sp) 7 times; repeat from ★ around, sc in first sc to form last ch-1 sp: 64 sc and 64 sps.

Rnd 10: Ch 1, sc in last ch-1 sp made and in next ch-3 sp, (ch 1, work FPsc around next sc, ch 1, sc in next ch-3 sp) 6 times, ★ sc in next 2 sps, (ch 1, work FPsc around next sc, ch 1, sc in next ch-3 sp) 6 times; repeat from ★ around; join with slip st to first sc: 112 sts and 96 ch-1 sps.

Rnd 11: Ch 1, working **behind** Rnd 10 and in same ch-3 sps on Rnd 9, sc in first ch-3 sp (before sc), ch 3, (sc in next ch-3 sp, ch 3) around; join with slip st to first sc: 56 ch-3 sps.

Rnd 12: (Slip st, ch 1, 2 sc) in first ch-3 sp, ch 2, (2 sc in next ch-3 sp, ch 2) around; join with slip st to first sc.

Rnd 13: Slip st in next sc and in next ch-2 sp, ch 1, sc in same sp, ch 2, 5 dc in next ch-2 sp, ch 2, ★ sc in next ch-2 sp, ch 2, 5 dc in next ch-2 sp, ch 2; repeat from ★ around; join with slip st to first sc: 28 5-dc groups and 56 ch-2 sps.

Rnd 14: (Slip st, ch 1, sc) in first ch-2 sp, ch 1, skip next 2 dc, work FPsc around next dc, ch 1, sc in next ch-2 sp, ch 3, ★ sc in next ch-2 sp, ch 1, skip next 2 dc, work FPsc around next dc, ch 1, sc in next ch-2 sp, ch 3; repeat from ★ around; join with slip st to first sc: 84 sps.

Rnd 15: (Slip st, ch 1, sc) in first ch-1 sp, ch 3, sc in next ch-1 sp, 5 dc in next ch-3 sp, ★ sc in next ch-1 sp, ch 3, sc in next ch-1 sp, 5 dc in next ch-3 sp; repeat from ★ around; join with slip st to first sc: 196 sts and 28 ch-3 sps.

Rnd 16: Ch 1, ★ skip next ch-3 sp and next sc, work FPsc around next dc, (ch 2, work FPsc around next dc) 4 times; repeat from ★ around; join with slip st to first FPsc: 140 FPsc and 112 ch-2 sps.

Rnd 17: Working **behind** Rnd 16 and in sts and sps on Rnd 15, slip st in first 5 dc and in next ch-3 sp, ch 3, (2 dc, ch 2, 3 dc) in same sp, ch 1, ★ (3 dc, ch 2, 3 dc) in next ch-3 sp, ch 1; repeat from ★ around; join with slip st to first dc: 168 dc and 56 sps.

Rnd 18: Slip st in next 2 dc and in next ch-2 sp, ch 3, (2 dc, ch 2, 3 dc) in same sp, ★ † ch 1, work First Leg of Split FPtr around center dc of next 3-dc group, skip next ch-1 sp, work Second Leg around center dc of next 3-dc group, ch 1 †, (3 dc, ch 2, 3 dc) in next ch-2 sp; repeat from ★ 26 times **more**, then repeat from † to † once; join with slip st to first dc: 196 sts and 84 sps.

Rnd 19: Slip st in next 2 dc and in next ch-2 sp, ch 3, (2 dc, ch 2, 3 dc) in same sp, ★ † ch 1, work First Leg of Split FPtr around center dc of next 3-dc group, skip next 2 ch-1 sps, work Second Leg around center dc of next 3-dc group, ch 1 †, (3 dc, ch 2, 3 dc) in next ch-2 sp; repeat from ★ 26 times **more**, then repeat from † to † once; join with slip st to first dc.

Rnd 20: Slip st in next 2 dc, ch 3, ★ † 5 dc in next ch-2 sp, dc in next dc, ch 1, work First Leg of Split FPtr around next dc, skip next 2 ch-1 sps and next dc, work Second Leg around next dc, ch 1 †, dc in next dc; repeat from ★ 26 times **more**, then repeat from † to † once; join with slip st to first dc: 224 sts and 56 ch-1 sps.

Rnd 21: Ch 1, sc in same st, work FPsc around next dc, (ch 2, work FPsc around next dc) 4 times, sc in next dc, ★ ch 3, skip next 2 ch-1 sps, sc in next dc, work FPsc around next dc, (ch 2, work FPsc around next dc) 4 times, sc in next dc; repeat from ★ around to last 2 ch-1 sps, skip last 2 ch-1 sps, dc in first sc to form last ch-3 sp: 140 sps.

Rnd 22: Ch 3, (2 dc, ch 3, 3 dc) in last ch-3 sp made, ch 5, skip next 4 ch-2 sps, ★ (3 dc, ch 3, 3 dc) in next ch-3 sp, ch 5, skip next 4 ch-2 sps; repeat from ★ around; join with slip st to first dc: 168 dc and 56 sps.

Rnd 23: Slip st in next 2 dc and in next ch-3 sp, ch 3, (2 dc, ch 3, 3 dc) in same sp, ★ † skip next dc, work FPtr around next dc, ch 1, slip st in next ch-5 sp, ch 1, skip next dc, work FPtr around next dc †, (3 dc, ch 3, 3 dc) in next ch-3 sp; repeat from ★ 26 times **more**, then repeat from † to † once; join with slip st to first dc: 252 sts and 84 sps.

Rnd 24: Ch 3, ★ † work FPtr around next dc, dc in next dc, (3 dc, ch 3, 3 dc) in next ch-3 sp, dc in next dc, work FPtr around next dc, dc in next dc, work First Leg of Split FPtr around next FPtr, skip next slip st, work Second Leg around next FPtr †, dc in next dc; repeat from ★ 26 times **more**, then repeat from † to † once; join with slip st to first dc: 364 sts and 28 ch-3 sps.

Rnd 25: Slip st in next 3 sts, ch 3, ★ † work FPtr around next dc, dc in next dc, 7 dc in next ch-3 sp, dc in next dc, work FPtr around next dc, dc in next dc, ch 1, skip next dc, work First Leg of Split FPtr around next FPtr, skip next 3 sts, work Second Leg around next FPtr, ch 1, skip next dc †, dc in next dc; repeat from ★ 26 times **more**, then repeat from † to † once; join with slip st to first dc: 392 sts and 56 ch-1 sps.

Rnd 26: Working in Back Loops Only, slip st in next 2 sts, ch 4, dc in next dc, (ch 1, dc in next dc) 7 times, ★ † work First Leg of Split FPtr around next FPtr, skip next 2 ch-1 sps and next dc, work Second Leg around next FPtr †, dc in next dc, (ch 1, dc in next dc) 8 times; repeat from ★ 26 times **more**, then repeat from † to † once; join with slip st to third ch of beginning ch-4: 224 ch-1 sps.

Rnd 27: (Slip st, ch 1, sc) in first ch-1 sp, (ch 3, sc in next ch-1 sp) 7 times, ★ ch 1, sc in next ch-1 sp, (ch 3, sc in next ch-1 sp) 7 times; repeat from ★ around, sc in first sc to form last ch-1 sp.

Rnd 28: Ch 1, sc in last ch-1 sp made and in next ch-3 sp, (ch 1, work FPsc around next sc, ch 1, sc in next ch-3 sp) 6 times, ★ sc in next 2 sps, (ch 1, work FPsc around next sc, ch 1, sc in next ch-3 sp) 6 times; repeat from ★ around; join with slip st to first sc, finish off.

See Washing and Blocking, page 2.

Extraordinary

EXPERIENCED

Finished Size: 16" (40.5 cm) from straight edge to straight edge

MATERIALS

Bedspread Weight Cotton Thread (size 10) [350 yards (320 meters) per ball]: Two balls
Steel crochet hook, size 7 (1.65 mm) **or** size needed for gauge

GAUGE SWATCH: 2⅝" (6.75 cm) diameter
Work same as Doily, page 9, through Rnd 4.

Stitch Guide

TREBLE CROCHET ***(abbreviated tr)***
YO twice, insert hook in sp indicated, YO and pull up a loop (4 loops on hook), (YO and draw through 2 loops on hook) 3 times.

BACK POST TREBLE CROCHET ***(abbreviated BPtr)***
YO twice, insert hook from **back** to **front** around post of dc indicated ***(Fig. 2, page 1)***, YO and pull up a loop (4 loops on hook), (YO and draw through 2 loops on hook) 3 times.

FRONT POST TREBLE CROCHET ***(abbreviated FPtr)***
YO twice, insert hook from **front** to **back** around post of dc indicated ***(Fig. 2, page 1)***, YO and pull up a loop (4 loops on hook), (YO and draw through 2 loops on hook) 3 times.

SPLIT FRONT POST TREBLE CROCHET ***(abbreviated Split FPtr)***
First Leg: YO twice, insert hook from **front** to **back** around post of st indicated ***(Fig. 2, page 1)***, YO and pull up a loop, (YO and draw through 2 loops on hook) twice (2 loops remaining on hook).
Second Leg: YO twice, insert hook from **front** to **back** around post of st indicated, YO and pull up a loop, (YO and draw through 2 loops on hook) twice, YO and draw through all 3 loops on hook.

Instructions continued on page 9.

DOILY

Ch 6; join with slip st to form a ring.

Rnd 1 (Right side)**:** Ch 5 **(counts as first dc plus ch 2)**, (2 dc in ring, ch 2) 7 times, dc in ring; join with slip st to first dc: 16 dc and 8 ch-2 sps.

Rnd 2: Ch 1, sc in same st, ch 2, 3 dc in next ch-2 sp, ch 2, skip next dc, ★ sc in next dc, ch 2, 3 dc in next ch-2 sp, ch 2, skip next dc; repeat from ★ around; join with slip st to first sc: 32 sts and 16 ch-2 sps.

Rnd 3: Ch 1, sc in same st, ★ ch 5, skip next 3 dc, sc in next sc; repeat from ★ around to last 3 dc, ch 2, skip last 3 dc, dc in first sc to form last ch-5 sp: 8 sc and 8 ch-5 sps.

Rnd 4: Ch 3 **(counts as first dc, now and throughout)**, 2 dc in last ch-5 sp made, working in **front** of Rnd 3, tr in next 2 ch-2 sps on Rnd 2, ★ (3 dc, ch 2, 3 dc) in next ch-5 sp on Rnd 3, working in **front** of Rnd 2, tr in next 2 ch-2 sps on Rnd 2; repeat from ★ around, 3 dc in same sp as first dc, ch 1, sc in first dc to form last ch-2 sp: 64 sts and 8 ch-2 sps.

Rnd 5: Ch 3, 2 dc in last ch-2 sp made, ★ † ch 1, skip next dc, work BPtr around next dc, skip next dc, work First Leg of Split FPtr around next tr, work Second Leg around next tr, skip next dc, work BPtr around next dc, ch 1 †, (3 dc, ch 2, 3 dc) in next ch-2 sp; repeat from ★ 6 times **more**, then repeat from † to † once, 3 dc in same sp as first dc, ch 1, sc in first dc to form last ch-2 sp: 72 sts and 24 sps.

Rnd 6: Ch 3, 2 dc in last ch-2 sp made, ch 2, ★ † skip next dc, work BPtr around next dc, skip next dc, work First Leg of Split FPtr around next BPtr, skip next Split FPtr, work Second Leg around next BPtr, skip next dc, work BPtr around next dc, ch 2 †, (3 dc, ch 2) twice in next ch-2 sp; repeat from ★ 6 times **more**, then repeat from † to † once, 3 dc in same sp as first dc, ch 1, sc in first dc to form last ch-2 sp.

Rnd 7: Ch 3, dc in last ch-2 sp made, ★ † dc in next dc, work FPtr around next dc, dc in next dc, 2 dc in next ch-2 sp, work First Leg of Split FPtr around next BPtr, skip next Split FPtr, work Second Leg around next BPtr, 2 dc in next ch-2 sp, dc in next dc, work FPtr around next dc, dc in next dc †, 3 dc in next ch-2 sp; repeat from ★ 6 times **more**, then repeat from † to † once, dc in same sp as first dc; join with slip st to first dc: 112 sts.

Rnd 8: Ch 1, sc in same st and in each st around; join with slip st to first sc.

Rnd 9: Ch 3, dc in same st, ch 1, skip next sc, ★ 2 dc in next sc, ch 1, skip next sc; repeat from ★ around; join with slip st to first dc: 112 dc and 56 ch-1 sps.

Rnd 10: Ch 3, dc in next dc, ch 1, (dc in next 2 dc, ch 1) around; join with slip st to first dc.

Rnd 11: Ch 3, dc in next dc, ch 1, dc in next 2 dc, ch 2, ★ dc in next 2 dc, ch 1, dc in next 2 dc, ch 2; repeat from ★ around; join with slip st to first dc.

Rnd 12: Ch 3, dc in next dc, ch 2, (dc in next 2 dc, ch 2) around; join with slip st to first dc.

Rnd 13: (Slip st, ch 3, dc) in next dc, ch 1, dc in next 2 dc, (ch 2, dc in next 2 dc) 5 times, ch 1, ★ 2 dc in next dc, ch 2, 2 dc in next dc, ch 1, dc in next 2 dc, (ch 2, dc in next 2 dc) 5 times, ch 1; repeat from ★ around to last st, 2 dc in last st, ch 1, sc in first dc to form last ch-2 sp: 128 dc.

Rnd 14: Ch 4 **(counts as first dc plus ch 1, now and throughout)**, (dc in next 2 dc, ch 1) twice, (dc in next 2 dc, ch 2) 3 times, (dc in next 2 dc, ch 1) 3 times, ★ 2 dc in next ch-2 sp, (ch 1, dc in next 2 dc) 3 times, ch 2, (dc in next 2 dc, ch 2) twice, (dc in next 2 dc, ch 1) 3 times; repeat from ★ around, dc in same sp as first dc; join with slip st to first dc: 144 dc.

Rnd 15: Ch 3, dc in same st, (ch 1, dc in next 2 dc) 4 times, ch 2, (dc in next 2 dc, ch 1) 4 times, 2 dc in next dc, ★ ch 2, 2 dc in next dc, (ch 1, dc in next 2 dc) 4 times, ch 2, (dc in next 2 dc, ch 1) 4 times, 2 dc in next dc; repeat from ★ around, ch 1, sc in first dc to form last ch-2 sp: 160 dc.

Rnd 16: Ch 4, (dc in next 2 dc, ch 1) 10 times, ★ 2 dc in next ch-2 sp, ch 1, (dc in next 2 dc, ch 1) 10 times; repeat from ★ around, dc in same sp as first dc; join with slip st to first dc: 176 dc.

Rnd 17: Ch 3, dc in same st and in next 2 dc, (ch 1, dc in next 2 dc) 9 times, 2 dc in next dc, ★ ch 2, 2 dc in next dc, dc in next 2 dc, (ch 1, dc in next 2 dc) 9 times, 2 dc in next dc; repeat from ★ around, ch 1, sc in first dc to form last ch-2 sp: 192 dc.

Rnd 18: Ch 3, ★ † dc in next 6 dc, ch 1, (dc in next 2 dc, ch 1) 6 times, dc in next 6 dc †, 2 dc in next ch-2 sp; repeat from ★ 6 times **more**, then repeat from † to † once, dc in same sp as first dc; join with slip st to first dc: 208 dc.

Rnd 19: Ch 3, dc in same st and in next 8 dc, ★ † ch 1, (dc in next 2 dc, ch 1) 4 times, dc in next 8 dc, 2 dc in next dc †, ch 2, 2 dc in next dc, dc in next 8 dc; repeat from ★ 6 times **more**, then repeat from † to † once, ch 1, sc in first dc to form last ch-2 sp: 224 dc.

Rnd 20: Ch 3, ★ † 2 dc in next dc, dc in next 11 dc, ch 1, (dc in next 2 dc, ch 1) twice, dc in next 11 dc †, 2 dc in next dc and in next ch-2 sp; repeat from ★ 6 times **more**, then repeat from † to † once, 2 dc last dc, dc in same sp as first dc; join with slip st to first dc: 256 dc.

Rnd 21: Ch 3, dc in same st and in next 15 dc, ch 1, dc in next 15 dc, 2 dc in next dc, ★ ch 2, 2 dc in next dc, dc in next 15 dc, ch 1, dc in next 15 dc, 2 dc in next dc; repeat from ★ around, ch 1, sc in first dc to form last ch-2 sp: 272 dc.

Rnd 22: Ch 3, 2 dc in next dc, dc in next 32 dc, 2 dc in next dc, ★ 2 dc in next ch-2 sp and in next dc, dc in next 32 dc, 2 dc in next dc; repeat from ★ around, dc in same sp as first dc; join with slip st to first dc: 304 dc.

Rnd 23: Ch 3, dc in same st and in next 36 dc, 2 dc in next dc, ★ ch 2, 2 dc in next dc, dc in next 36 dc, 2 dc in next dc; repeat from ★ around, ch 1, sc in first dc to form last ch-2 sp: 320 dc and 8 ch-2 sps.

Rnd 24: Ch 1, 2 sc in last ch-2 sp made, sc in next 40 dc, (3 sc in next ch-2 sp, sc in next 40 dc) around, sc in same sp as first sc; join with slip st to first sc: 344 sc.

Rnd 25: Ch 3, dc in same st, ★ † skip next sc, dc in next sc, skip next sc, (dc, ch 1, dc) in next sc, skip next sc, [dc in next 2 sc, skip next sc, (dc, ch 1, dc) in next sc, skip next sc] 7 times, dc in next sc, skip next sc †, (2 dc, ch 2, 2 dc) in next sc; repeat from ★ 6 times **more**, then repeat from † to † once, 2 dc in same st as first dc, ch 2; join with slip st to first dc: 288 dc and 72 sps.

Rnd 26: Slip st in next dc, ch 1, sc in same st and in next dc, ★ † (5 tr in next ch-1 sp, skip next dc, sc in next 2 dc) 8 times, 7 tr in next ch-2 sp †, skip next dc, sc in next 2 dc; repeat from ★ 6 times **more**, then repeat from † to † once, skip next st; join with slip st to first sc, finish off.

See Washing and Blocking, page 2.

Expressive

EXPERIENCED

Finished Size: 13¼" (33.5 cm) diameter

MATERIALS

Bedspread Weight Cotton Thread (size 10) [350 yards (320 meters) per ball]: One ball
Steel crochet hook, size 7 (1.65 mm) **or** size needed for gauge

GAUGE SWATCH: 1¾" (4.5 cm) diameter
Work same as Doily, page 13, through Rnd 4.

Stitch Guide

FRONT POST SINGLE CROCHET ***(abbreviated FPsc)***
Insert hook from **front** to **back** around post of FPtr indicated ***(Fig. 2, page 1)***, YO and pull up a loop, YO and draw through both loops on hook.

FRONT POST TREBLE CROCHET ***(abbreviated FPtr)***
YO twice, insert hook from **front** to **back** around post of dc indicated ***(Fig. 2, page 1)***, YO and pull up a loop (4 loops on hook), (YO and draw through 2 loops on hook) 3 times.

SPLIT FRONT POST SINGLE CROCHET ***(abbreviated Split FPsc)*** (uses next 2 FPtr)
★ Insert hook from **front** to **back** around post of **next** FPtr ***(Fig. 2, page 1)***, YO and pull up a loop; repeat from ★ once **more**, YO and draw through all 3 loops on hook.

SPLIT FRONT POST DOUBLE CROCHET ***(abbreviated Split FPdc)***
★ YO, insert hook from **front** to **back** around post of **next** FPtr ***(Fig. 2, page 1)***, YO and pull up a loop, YO and draw through 2 loops on hook; repeat from ★ once **more**, YO and draw through all 3 loops on hook.

SPLIT FRONT POST TREBLE CROCHET ***(abbreviated Split FPtr)***
First Leg: YO twice, insert hook from **front** to **back** around post of dc indicated ***(Fig. 2, page 1)***, YO and pull up a loop, (YO and draw through 2 loops on hook) twice (2 loops remaining on hook).
Second Leg: YO twice, insert hook from **front** to **back** around post dc indicated, YO and pull up a loop, (YO and draw through 2 loops on hook) twice, YO and draw through all 3 loops on hook.

Instructions continued on page 13.

With Best Wishe

BEGINNING CLUSTER (uses one st or sp)
Ch 2, ★ YO, insert hook in st or sp indicated, YO and pull up a loop, YO and draw through 2 loops on hook; repeat from ★ once **more**, YO and draw through all 3 loops on hook.
CLUSTER (uses one st or sp)
★ YO, insert hook in st or sp indicated, YO and pull up a loop, YO and draw through 2 loops on hook; repeat from ★ 2 times **more**, YO and draw through all 4 loops on hook.

SPLIT CLUSTER (uses 4 sts and one ch-1 sp)
YO twice, † insert hook from **front** to **back** around post of **next** FPtr ***(Fig. 2, page 1)***, YO and pull up a loop, (YO and draw through 2 loops on hook) twice †, YO, skip next dc, insert hook in next ch-1 sp, YO and pull up a loop, YO and draw through 2 loops on hook (3 loops remaining on hook), YO twice, skip next dc, repeat from † to † once, YO and draw through all 4 loops on hook.
DECREASE (uses next 3 dc)
Beginning in dc indicated, ★ YO, insert hook in **next** dc, YO and pull up a loop, YO and draw through 2 loops on hook; repeat from ★ 2 times **more**, YO and draw through all 4 loops on hook.

DOILY

Ch 6; join with slip st to form a ring.

Rnd 1 (Right side)**:** Ch 5 **(counts as first dc plus ch 2, now and throughout)**, (2 dc in ring, ch 2) 7 times, dc in ring; join with slip st to first dc: 16 dc and 8 ch-2 sps.

Rnd 2: Slip st in first ch-2 sp, ch 3 **(counts as first dc, now and throughout)**, 3 dc in same sp, ch 1, (4 dc in next ch-2 sp, ch 1) around; join with slip st to first dc: 32 dc and 8 ch-1 sps.

Rnd 3: Ch 1, sc in same st and in next dc, working in **front** of Rnd 2, work FPtr around first dc on Rnd 1 and around next dc, sc in next 2 dc on Rnd 2 and in next ch-1 sp, ★ sc in next 2 dc, working in **front** of Rnd 2, work FPtr around each of next 2 dc on Rnd 1, sc in next 2 dc on Rnd 2 and in next ch-1 sp; repeat from ★ around; join with slip st to first sc: 56 sts.

Rnd 4: Ch 1, sc in same st and in next sc, work Split FPsc, (sc in next 5 sc, work Split FPsc) around to last 3 sc, sc in last 3 sc; join with slip st to first sc: 48 sts.

Rnd 5: Ch 3, dc in next sc, 3 dc in next Split FPsc, (dc in next 5 sc, 3 dc in next Split FPsc) around to last 3 sc, dc in last 3 sc; join with slip st to first dc: 64 dc.

Rnd 6: (Slip st, work Beginning Cluster) in next dc, ch 2, skip next dc, ★ work Cluster in next dc, ch 2, skip next st; repeat from ★ around; join with slip st to top of Beginning Cluster: 32 Clusters and 32 ch-2 sps.

Rnd 7: Ch 1, sc in same st, 2 sc in next ch-2 sp, working in **front** of Rnd 6, work FPtr around first skipped dc on Rnd 5 and around next skipped dc, 2 sc in next ch-2 sp on Rnd 6, ★ sc in next Cluster, 2 sc in next ch-2 sp, working in **front** of Rnd 6, work FPtr around each of next 2 skipped dc on Rnd 5, 2 sc in next ch-2 sp on Rnd 6; repeat from ★ around; join with slip st to first sc: 112 sts.

Rnd 8: Ch 1, sc in same st and in next 2 sc, work Split FPsc, (sc in next 5 sc, work Split FPsc) around to last 2 sc, sc in last 2 sc; join with slip st to first sc: 96 sts.

Rnd 9: Ch 3, dc in next 2 sc, 3 dc in next Split FPsc, (dc in next 5 sc, 3 dc in next Split FPsc) around to last 2 sc, dc in last 2 sc; join with slip st to first dc: 128 dc.

Rnd 10: Work Beginning Cluster in same st, ch 2, skip next dc, ★ work Cluster in next dc, ch 2, skip next dc; repeat from ★ around; join with slip st to top of Beginning Cluster: 64 Clusters and 64 ch-2 sps.

Rnd 11: Ch 1, sc in same st and in next ch-2 sp, working in **front** of Rnd 10, work FPtr around first skipped dc on Rnd 9 and around next skipped dc, sc in next ch-2 sp on Rnd 10, ★ sc in next Cluster and in next ch-2 sp, working in **front** of Rnd 10, work FPtr around each of next 2 skipped dc on Rnd 9, sc in next ch-2 sp on Rnd 10; repeat from ★ around; join with slip st to first sc: 160 sts.

Rnd 12: Ch 5, dc in same st, skip next sc, work Split FPdc, skip next sc, ★ (dc, ch 2, dc) in next sc, skip next sc, work Split FPdc, skip next sc; repeat from ★ around; join with slip st to first dc: 96 sts and 32 ch-2 sps.

Rnd 13: Slip st in first ch-2 sp, ch 4 **(counts as first dc plus ch 1)**, dc in same sp, work FPtr around next dc, (dc, ch 1, dc) in next Split FPdc, work FPtr around next dc, ★ (dc, ch 1, dc) in next ch-2 sp, work FPtr around next dc, (dc, ch 1, dc) in next Split FPdc, work FPtr around next dc; repeat from ★ around; join with slip st to first dc: 192 sts and 64 ch-1 sps.

Rnd 14: (Slip st, ch 3, dc, ch 2, 2 dc) in first ch-1 sp, skip next dc, work Split Cluster, ★ (2 dc, ch 2, 2 dc) in next ch-1 sp, skip next dc, work Split Cluster; repeat from ★ around; join with slip st to first dc: 160 sts and 32 ch-2 sps.

Rnd 15: Slip st in next dc and in next ch-2 sp, ch 3, (2 dc, ch 2, 3 dc) in same sp, skip next dc, work First Leg of Split FPtr around next dc, skip next Split Cluster, work Second Leg around next dc, ★ (3 dc, ch 2, 3 dc) in next ch-1 sp, skip next dc, work First Leg of Split FPtr around next dc, skip next Split Cluster, work Second Leg around next dc; repeat from ★ around; join with slip st to first dc: 224 sts and 32 ch-2 sps.

Rnd 16: Slip st in next 2 dc and in next ch-2 sp, work Beginning Cluster in same sp, ★ † (ch 2, work Cluster in same sp) twice, ch 1, skip next dc, work First Leg of Split FPtr around next dc, skip next 3 sts, work Second Leg around next dc, ch 1 †, work Cluster in next ch-2 sp; repeat from ★ 30 times **more**, then repeat from † to † once; join with slip st to top of Beginning Cluster: 128 sps.

Rnd 17: Work (slip st, Beginning Cluster, ch 2, Cluster) in first ch-2 sp, (ch 2, work Cluster) twice in next ch-2 sp, skip next 2 ch-1 sps, ★ work (Cluster, ch 2, Cluster) in next ch-2 sp, (ch 2, work Cluster) twice in next ch-2 sp, skip next 2 ch-1 sps; repeat from ★ around; join with slip st to top of Beginning Cluster: 96 ch-2 sps.

Rnd 18: (Slip st, work Beginning Cluster) in first ch-2 sp, ch 1, work Cluster in next ch-2 sp, (ch 2, work Cluster in same sp) twice, ch 1, ★ work Cluster in next 2 ch-2 sps, ch 1, work Cluster in next ch-2 sp, (ch 2, work Cluster in same sp) twice, ch 1; repeat from ★ around to last ch-2 sp, work Cluster in last ch-2 sp; join with slip st to top of Beginning Cluster: 160 Clusters and 128 sps.

Rnd 19: Ch 5, dc in same st, skip next ch-1 sp, 3 dc in next ch-2 sp, dc in next Cluster, 3 dc in next ch-2 sp, skip next 2 Clusters, ★ (dc, ch 2, dc) in next Cluster, skip next ch-1 sp, 3 dc in next ch-2 sp, dc in next Cluster, 3 dc in next ch-2 sp, skip next 2 Clusters; repeat from ★ around; join with slip st to first dc: 288 sts and 32 ch-2 sps.

Rnd 20: (Slip st, ch 5, dc) in first ch-2 sp, ★ † work FPtr around next dc, decrease beginning in next dc, work FPtr around last dc used, (dc, ch 2, dc) in next dc, work FPtr around next dc, decrease beginning in last dc used (behind FPtr), work FPtr around next dc †, (dc ch 2, dc) in next ch-2 sp; repeat from ★ 30 times **more**, then repeat from † to † once; join with slip st to first dc: 320 sts and 64 ch-2 sps.

Instructions continued on page 19.

Exceptional

Shown on Front Cover.

EXPERIENCED

Finished Size: 13" (33 cm) diameter

MATERIALS

Bedspread Weight Cotton Thread (size 10) [400 yards (366 meters) per ball]: One ball

Steel crochet hook, size 7 (1.65 mm) **or** size needed for gauge

GAUGE SWATCH: 2¼" (5.75 cm) diameter

Work same as Doily, page 17, through Rnd 4.

Stitch Guide

BEGINNING CLUSTER (uses one st or sp)
Ch 2, ★ YO, insert hook in **same** st or sp, YO and pull up a loop, YO and draw through 2 loops on hook; repeat from ★ once **more**, YO and draw through all 3 loops on hook.

CLUSTER (uses one st or sp)
★ YO, insert hook in st or sp indicated, YO and pull up a loop, YO and draw through 2 loops on hook; repeat from ★ 2 times **more**, YO and draw through all 4 loops on hook.

FRONT POST SINGLE CROCHET ***(abbreviated FPsc)***
Insert hook from **front** to **back** around post of st indicated ***(Fig. 2, page 1)***, YO and pull up a loop, YO and draw through both loops on hook.

FRONT POST DOUBLE CROCHET ***(abbreviated FPdc)***
YO, insert hook from **front** to **back** around post of st indicated ***(Fig. 2, page 1)***, YO and pull up a loop (3 loops on hook), (YO and draw through 2 loops on hook) twice.

BACK POST DOUBLE CROCHET ***(abbreviated BPdc)***
YO, insert hook from **back** to **front** around post of FPtr indicated ***(Fig. 2, page 1)***, YO and pull up a loop (3 loops on hook), (YO and draw through 2 loops on hook) twice.

FRONT POST TREBLE CROCHET ***(abbreviated FPtr)***
YO twice, insert hook from **front** to **back** around post of st indicated ***(Fig. 2, page 1)***, YO and pull up a loop (4 loops on hook), (YO and draw through 2 loops on hook) 3 times.

SPLIT FRONT POST TREBLE CROCHET ***(abbreviated Split FPtr)*** (uses next 3 sts)
YO twice, † insert hook from **front** to **back** around post of **next** FPtr ***(Fig. 2, page 1)***, YO and pull up a loop, (YO and draw through 2 loops on hook) twice †, YO twice, skip next Cluster, repeat from † to † once, YO and draw through all 3 loops on hook.

DECREASE (uses next 4 FPtr)
★ YO twice, insert hook from **front** to **back** around post of **next** FPtr ***(Fig. 2, page 1)***, YO and pull up a loop, (YO and draw through 2 loops on hook) twice; repeat from ★ 3 times **more**, YO and draw through all 5 loops on hook.

Instructions continued on page 17.

DOILY

Ch 6; join with slip st to form a ring.

Rnd 1 (Right side)**:** Ch 3 **(counts as first dc, now and throughout),** 2 dc in ring, (ch 2, 3 dc in ring) 5 times, hdc in first dc to form last ch-2 sp: 18 dc and 6 ch-2 sps.

Rnd 2: Work (Beginning Cluster, ch 2, Cluster) in last ch-2 sp made, ch 1, skip next dc, work FPtr around next dc, ch 1, ★ work (Cluster, ch 2, Cluster) in next ch-2 sp, ch 1, skip next dc, work FPtr around next dc, ch 1; repeat from ★ around; join with slip st to top of Beginning Cluster: 18 sts and 18 sps.

Rnd 3: (Slip st, ch 3, 4 dc) in first ch-2 sp, 2 dc in next ch-1 sp, work FPtr around next FPtr, 2 dc in next ch-1 sp, ★ 5 dc in next ch-2 sp, 2 dc in next ch-1 sp, work FPtr around next FPtr, 2 dc in next ch-1 sp; repeat from ★ around; join with slip st to first dc: 60 sts.

Rnd 4: Slip st in next dc, ★ work FPsc around next dc, ch 3, skip next 2 dc, sc in sp **before** next dc ***(Fig. 3)***, ch 3, skip next 2 dc, work FPsc around next FPtr, ch 3, skip next 2 sts, sc in sp **before** next dc, ch 3, skip next 2 sts; repeat from ★ around; join with slip st to first FPsc: 24 ch-3 sps.

Fig. 3

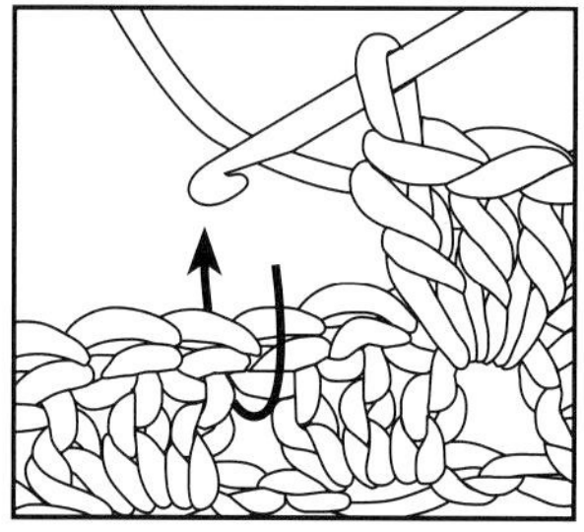

Rnd 5: (Slip st, ch 1, 3 sc) in first ch-3 sp, 3 sc in each ch-3 sp around; join with slip st to first sc: 72 sc.

Rnd 6: Ch 1, sc in same st and in each sc around; join with slip st to first sc.

Rnd 7: Ch 3, dc in next 2 sc, (ch 2, dc in next 3 sc) around, hdc in first dc to form last ch-2 sp: 72 dc and 24 ch-2 sps.

Rnd 8: Work (Beginning Cluster, ch 3, Cluster) in last ch-2 sp made, ch 1, skip next dc, work FPtr around next dc, ch 1, ★ work (Cluster, ch 3, Cluster) in next ch-2 sp, ch 1, skip next dc, work FPtr around next dc, ch 1; repeat from ★ around; join with slip st to top of Beginning Cluster: 72 sts and 72 sps.

Rnd 9: (Slip st, ch 3, dc, ch 2, 2 dc) in first ch-3 sp, skip next Cluster, work FPdc around next FPtr, skip next ch-1 sp, ★ (2 dc, ch 2, 2 dc) in next ch-3 sp, skip next Cluster, work FPdc around next FPtr, skip next ch-1 sp; repeat from ★ around; join with slip st to first dc: 120 sts and 24 ch-2 sps.

Rnd 10: Slip st in next dc and in next ch-2 sp, ch 3, (dc, ch 2, 2 dc) in same sp, skip next 2 dc, work FPdc around next FPdc, ★ (2 dc, ch 2, 2 dc) in next ch-2 sp, skip next 2 dc, work FPdc around next FPdc; repeat from ★ around; join with slip st to first dc.

Rnd 11: Slip st in next dc and in next ch-2 sp, ch 3, (2 dc, ch 2, 3 dc) in same sp, skip next 2 dc, work FPtr around next FPdc, ★ (3 dc, ch 2, 3 dc) in next ch-2 sp, skip next 2 dc, work FPtr around next FPdc; repeat from ★ around; join with slip st to first dc: 168 sts and 24 ch-2 sps.

Rnd 12: Slip st in next 2 dc and in next ch-2 sp, ch 3, (2 dc ch 3, 3 dc) in same sp, skip next 3 dc, work FPtr around next FPtr, ★ (3 dc, ch 3, 3 dc) in next ch-2 sp, skip next 3 dc, work FPtr around next FPtr; repeat from ★ around; join with slip st to first dc.

Rnd 13: Ch 2, work FPdc around each of next 2 dc, (skip next ch-3 sp, work FPdc around each of next 7 sts) around to last ch-3 sp, skip last ch-3 sp, work FPdc around each of last 5 sts; join with slip st to first FPdc.

Rnd 14: Ch 1, working **behind** Rnd 13 and in skipped ch-3 sps and around sts on Rnd 12, (slip st, ch 3, 8 dc) in first ch-3 sp, skip next 3 dc, work BPdc around next FPtr, ★ 9 dc in next ch-3 sp, skip next 3 dc, work BPdc around next FPtr; repeat from ★ around; join with slip st to first dc: 240 sts.

Rnd 15: Ch 1, sc in same st, (ch 3, skip next dc, sc in next dc) 4 times, skip next BPdc, ★ sc in next dc, (ch 3, skip next dc, sc in next dc) 4 times, skip next BPdc; repeat from ★ around; join with slip st to first sc: 96 ch-3 sps.

Rnd 16: (Slip st, ch 1, sc) in first ch-3 sp, (ch 3, sc in next ch-3 sp) 3 times, ch 1, ★ sc in next ch-3 sp, (ch 3, sc in next ch-3 sp) 3 times, ch 1; repeat from ★ around; join with slip st to first sc.

Rnd 17: (Slip st, ch 1, sc) in first ch-3 sp, (ch 3, sc in next ch-3 sp) twice, (dc, ch 2, dc) in next ch-1 sp, ★ sc in next ch-3 sp, (ch 3, sc in next ch-3 sp) twice, (dc, ch 2, dc) in next ch-1 sp; repeat from ★ around; join with slip st to first sc: 72 sps.

Rnd 18: (Slip st, ch 1, sc) in first ch-3 sp, ch 3, sc in next ch-3 sp, (2 dc, ch 2, 2 dc) in next ch-2 sp, ★ sc in next ch-3 sp, ch 3, sc in next ch-3 sp, (2 dc, ch 2, 2 dc) in next ch-2 sp; repeat from ★ around; join with slip st to first sc: 144 sts and 48 sps.

Rnd 19: (Slip st, ch 1, sc) in first ch-3 sp, skip next sc, work FPtr around each of next 2 dc, 7 dc in next ch-2 sp, work FPtr around each of next 2 dc, ★ sc in next ch-3 sp, skip next sc, work FPtr around each of next 2 dc, 7 dc in next ch-2 sp, work FPtr around each of next 2 dc; repeat from ★ around; join with slip st to first sc: 288 sts.

Rnd 20: Slip st in next 3 sts, work Beginning Cluster in same st, ★ † ch 1, (skip next dc, work Cluster in next dc, ch 1) 3 times, work FPtr around each of next 2 FPtr, skip next sc, work FPtr around each of next 2 FPtr †, ch 1, work Cluster in next dc; repeat from ★ 22 times **more**, then repeat from † to † once, sc in top of Beginning Cluster to form last ch-1 sp: 192 sts and 120 ch-1 sps.

Rnd 21: Work Beginning Cluster in last ch-1 sp made, ch 1, (work Cluster in next ch-1 sp, ch 1) 4 times, decrease, ★ ch 1, (work Cluster in next ch-1 sp, ch 1) 5 times, decrease; repeat from ★ around, sc in top of Beginning Cluster to form last ch-1 sp: 144 ch-1 sps.

Rnd 22: Work Beginning Cluster in last ch-1 sp made, (ch 2, work Cluster in next ch-1 sp) 5 times, ch 1, ★ work Cluster in next ch-1 sp, (ch 2, work Cluster in next ch-1 sp) 5 times, ch 1; repeat from ★ around; join with slip st to top of Beginning Cluster.

Rnd 23: (Slip st, work Beginning Cluster) in first ch-2 sp, (ch 2, work Cluster in next ch-2 sp) 4 times, (2 dc, ch 2, 2 dc) in next ch-1 sp, ★ work Cluster in next ch-2 sp, (ch 2, work Cluster in next ch-2 sp) 4 times, (2 dc, ch 2, 2 dc) in next ch-1 sp; repeat from ★ around; join with slip st to top of Beginning Cluster: 216 sts and 120 ch-2 sps.

Rnd 24: (Slip st, work Beginning Cluster) in first ch-2 sp, ★ † (ch 2, work Cluster in next ch-2 sp) 3 times, skip next Cluster, work FPtr around each of next 2 dc, (dc, ch 2, dc) in next ch-2 sp, work FPtr around each of next 2 dc †, work Cluster in next ch-2 sp; repeat from ★ 22 times **more**, then repeat from † to † once; join with slip st to top of Beginning Cluster: 240 sts and 96 ch-2 sps.

Rnd 25: (Slip st, work Beginning Cluster) in first ch-2 sp, ★ † (ch 2, work Cluster in next ch-2 sp) twice, skip next Cluster, work FPtr around each of next 3 sts, (dc, ch 2, dc) in next ch-2 sp, work FPtr around each of next 3 sts †, work Cluster in next ch-2 sp; repeat from ★ 22 times **more**, then repeat from † to † once; join with slip st to top of Beginning Cluster: 264 sts and 72 ch-2 sps.

Rnd 26: (Slip st, work Beginning Cluster) in first ch-2 sp, ★ † ch 2, work Cluster in next ch-2 sp, skip next Cluster, work FPtr around each of next 4 sts, (dc, ch 2, dc) in next ch-2 sp, work FPtr around each of next 4 sts †, work Cluster in next ch-2 sp; repeat from ★ 22 times **more**, then repeat from † to † once; join with slip st to top of Beginning Cluster: 288 sts and 48 ch-2 sps.

Rnd 27: (Slip st, work Beginning Cluster) in first ch-2 sp, ★ † skip next Cluster, work FPtr around each of next 5 sts, (2 dc, ch 2, 2 dc) in next ch-2 sp, work FPtr around each of next 5 sts †, work Cluster in next ch-2 sp; repeat from ★ 22 times **more**, then repeat from † to † once; join with slip st to top of Beginning Cluster: 360 sts and 24 ch-2 sps.

Instructions continued on page 19.

Rnd 28: Slip st in next FPtr and around post next FPtr, ch 4, work FPtr around each of next 5 sts, 3 dc in next ch-2 sp, work FPtr around each of next 6 sts, work Split FPtr, ★ work FPtr around each of next 6 sts, 3 dc in next ch-2 sp, work FPtr around each of next 6 sts, work Split FPtr; repeat from ★ around; join with slip st to fourth ch of beginning ch-4: 384 sts.

Rnd 29: Ch 1, sc in same st and in each st around; join with slip st to first sc, finish off.

See Washing and Blocking, page 2.

Expressive

Continued from page 14.

Rnd 21: (Slip st, ch 1, sc, ch 5, 2 sc) in first ch-2 sp, skip next dc, work FPsc around next FPtr, skip next decrease, work FPsc around next FPtr, ★ (2 sc, ch 5, 2 sc) in next ch-2 sp, skip next dc, work FPsc around next FPtr, skip next decrease, work FPsc around next FPtr; repeat from ★ around, sc in same sp as first sc; join with slip st to first sc: 384 sts and 64 ch-5 sps.

Rnd 22: Slip st in next 2 chs, ch 1, 2 sc in same ch-5 sp, dc in next sc, skip next 4 sts, dc in next sc, ★ 3 sc in next ch-5 sp, dc in next sc, skip next 4 sts, dc in next sc; repeat from ★ around, sc in same sp as first sc; join with slip st to first sc: 320 sts.

Rnd 23: Ch 3, dc in next sc and in each st around; join with slip st to first dc.

Rnd 24: Work Beginning Cluster in same st, ch 2, skip next dc, ★ work Cluster in next dc, ch 2, skip next dc; repeat from ★ around; join with slip st to top of Beginning Cluster: 160 Clusters and 160 ch-2 sps.

Rnd 25: Ch 1, sc in same st and in next ch-2 sp, working in **front** of Rnd 24, work FPtr around first skipped dc on Rnd 23 and around next skipped dc, sc in next ch-2 sp on Rnd 24, ★ sc in next Cluster and in next ch-2 sp, working in **front** of Rnd 24, work FPtr around each of next 2 skipped dc on Rnd 23, sc in next ch-2 sp on Rnd 24; repeat from ★ around; join with slip st to first sc: 400 sts.

Rnd 26: Ch 1, sc in same st and in next sc, work Split FPsc, (sc in next 3 sc, work Split FPsc) around to last sc, sc in last sc; join with slip st to first sc: 320 sts.

Rnd 27: Ch 1, sc in same st, ch 1, skip next sc, (sc, ch 3, sc) in next Split FPsc, ch 1, skip next sc, ★ sc in next sc, ch 1, skip next sc, (sc, ch 3, sc) in next Split FPsc, ch 1, skip next sc; repeat from ★ around; join with slip st to first sc, finish off.

See Washing and Blocking, page 2.

Exquisite

Shown on page 24.

EXPERIENCED

Finished Size: 15¼" (38.5 cm) diameter

MATERIALS

Bedspread Weight Cotton Thread (size 10) [350 yards (320 meters) per ball]: Two balls
Steel crochet hook, size 7 (1.65 mm) **or** size needed for gauge

GAUGE SWATCH: 2⅛" (5.5 cm) diameter
Work same as Doily, page 21, through Rnd 4.

Stitch Guide

TREBLE CROCHET ***(abbreviated tr)***
YO twice, insert hook in sc indicated, YO and pull up a loop (4 loops on hook), (YO and draw through 2 loops on hook) 3 times.

FRONT POST DOUBLE CROCHET ***(abbreviated FPdc)***
YO, insert hook from **front** to **back** around post of st indicated ***(Fig. 2, page 1)***, YO and pull up a loop (3 loops on hook), (YO and draw through 2 loops on hook) twice.

FRONT POST TREBLE CROCHET ***(abbreviated FPtr)***
YO twice, insert hook from **front** to **back** around post of st indicated ***(Fig. 2, page 1)***, YO and pull up a loop (4 loops on hook), (YO and draw through 2 loops on hook) 3 times.

SPLIT FRONT POST SINGLE CROCHET ***(abbreviated Split FPsc)***
★ Insert hook from **front** to **back** around post of **next** FPtr ***(Fig. 2, page 1)***, YO and pull up a loop; repeat from ★ once **more**, YO and draw through all 3 loops on hook.

SPLIT FRONT POST TREBLE CROCHET ***(abbreviated Split FPtr)***
First Leg: YO twice, insert hook from **front** to **back** around post of st indicated ***(Fig. 2, page 1)***, YO and pull up a loop, (YO and draw through 2 loops on hook) twice (2 loops remaining on hook).
Second Leg: YO twice, insert hook from **front** to **back** around post of st indicated, YO and pull up a loop, (YO and draw through 2 loops on hook) twice, YO and draw through all 3 loops on hook.

BEGINNING DECREASE (uses first 3 dc)
Ch 2, YO twice, insert hook from **front** to **back** around post of next dc ***(Fig. 2, page 1)***, YO and pull up a loop, (YO and draw through 2 loops on hook) twice, YO, insert hook in next dc, YO and pull up a loop, YO and draw through 2 loops on hook, YO and draw through all 3 loops on hook.

Instructions continued on page 21.

DECREASE (uses next 3 dc)
† YO, insert hook in **next** dc, YO and pull up a loop, YO and draw through 2 loops on hook †, YO twice, insert hook from **front** to **back** around post of next dc ***(Fig. 2, page 1)***, YO and pull up a loop, (YO and draw through 2 loops on hook) twice, repeat from † to † once, YO and draw through all 4 loops on hook.

DOUBLE DECREASE (uses next 6 sts)
† ★ YO twice, insert hook from **front** to **back** around post of **next** dc ***(Fig. 2, page 1)***, YO and pull up a loop, (YO and draw through 2 loops on hook) twice; repeat from ★ once **more** †, skip next 2 FPtr, repeat from † to † once, YO and draw through all 5 loops on hook.

DOILY

Ch 5; join with slip st to form a ring.

Rnd 1 (Right side): Ch 3 **(counts as first dc, now and throughout)**, dc in ring, (ch 1, 2 dc in ring) 7 times, sc in first dc to form last ch-1 sp: 16 dc and 8 ch-1 sps.

Rnd 2: Ch 3, 2 dc in last ch-1 sp made, work FPtr around each of next 2 dc, (3 dc in next ch-1 sp, work FPtr around each of next 2 dc) around; join with slip st to first dc: 40 sts.

Rnd 3: Ch 1, sc in same st and in next 2 dc, work Split FPsc, (sc in next 3 dc, work Split FPsc) around; join with slip st in first sc: 32 sts.

Rnd 4: Ch 1, sc in same st, ★ ch 5, skip next st, sc in next sc; repeat from ★ around to last st, ch 2, skip last st, dc in first sc to form last ch-5 sp: 16 ch-5 sps.

Rnd 5: Ch 1, sc in last ch-5 sp made, ch 5, (sc in next ch-5 sp, ch 5) around; join with slip st to first sc.

Rnd 6: (Slip st, ch 3, 2 dc, ch 2, 3 dc) in first ch-5 sp, (3 dc, ch 2, 3 dc) in each ch-5 sp around; join with slip st in first dc: 96 sts and 16 ch-2 sps.

Rnd 7: Work beginning decrease, (2 dc, ch 2, 2 dc) in next ch-2 sp, decrease, ch 3, ★ decrease, (2 dc, ch 2, 2 dc) in next ch-2 sp, decrease, ch 3; repeat from ★ around; join with slip st to top of beginning decrease: 96 sts and 32 sps.

Rnd 8: Ch 1, sc in same st and in next 2 dc, (sc, ch 3, sc) in next ch-2 sp, ★ sc in next 3 sts, (sc, ch 3, sc) in next sp; repeat from ★ around; join with slip st to first sc: 160 sts and 32 ch-3 sps.

Doily may ruffle but will lay flat after subsequent rounds.

Rnd 9: (Slip st, ch 1, sc) in next sc, ★ ch 7, skip next ch-3 sp and next 2 sc, sc in next sc; repeat from ★ around to last ch-3 sp, ch 3, skip last ch-3 sp and last 2 sts, tr in first sc to form last ch-7 sp.

Rnd 10: Ch 1, sc in last ch-7 sp made, (ch 7, sc in next ch-7 sp) around, ch 3, tr in first sc to form last ch-7 sp.

Rnd 11: Ch 3, 2 dc in top of last tr made, (3 dc, ch 2, 3 dc) in center ch of each ch-7 around, 3 dc in same st as first dc, ch 1, sc in first dc to form last ch-2 sp: 192 dc and 32 ch-2 sps.

Rnd 12: Ch 3, 2 dc in last ch-2 sp made, skip next dc, work First Leg of Split FPtr around next dc, skip next 2 dc, work Second Leg around next dc, ★ (3 dc, ch 2, 3 dc) in next ch-2 sp, skip next dc, work First Leg of Split FPtr around next dc, skip next 2 dc, work Second Leg around next dc; repeat from ★ around, 3 dc in same sp as first dc, ch 1, sc in first dc to form last ch-2 sp: 224 sts and 32 ch-2 sps.

Rnd 13: Ch 3, 2 dc in last ch-2 sp made, skip next dc, work FPtr around next dc, skip next 3 sts, work FPtr around next dc, ★ (3 dc, ch 2, 3 dc) in next ch-2 sp, skip next dc, work FPtr around next dc, skip next 3 sts, work FPtr around next dc; repeat from ★ around, 3 dc in same sp as first dc, ch 1, sc in first dc to form last ch-2 sp: 256 sts and 32 ch-2 sps.

Rnd 14: Ch 3, 2 dc in last ch-2 sp made, skip next dc, work FPtr around next dc, skip next 4 sts, work FPtr around next dc, ★ (3 dc, ch 2, 3 dc) in next ch-2 sp, skip next dc, work FPtr around next dc, skip next 4 sts, work FPtr around next dc; repeat from ★ around, 3 dc in same sp as first dc, ch 1, sc in first dc to form last ch-2 sp.

Rnd 15: Ch 3, 2 dc in last ch-2 sp made, ch 1, skip next dc, double decrease, ch 1, 7 dc in next ch-2 sp, ch 1, skip next dc, double decrease, ch 1, ★ (3 dc, ch 2, 3 dc) in next ch-2 sp, ch 1, skip next dc, double decrease, ch 1, 7 dc in next ch-2 sp, ch 1, skip next dc, double decrease, ch 1; repeat from ★ around, 3 dc in same sp as first dc, ch 1, sc in first dc to form last ch-2 sp: 240 sts and 80 sps.

Rnd 16: Ch 3, 2 dc in last ch-2 sp made, ★ † skip next dc, work FPtr around next dc, ch 1, skip next 2 ch-1 sps, (dc in next dc, ch 1) 7 times, skip next 2 ch-1 sps and next dc, work FPtr around next dc †, (3 dc, ch 2, 3 dc) in next ch-2 sp; repeat from ★ 14 times **more**, then repeat from † to † once, 3 dc in same sp as first dc, ch 1, sc in first dc to form last ch-2 sp: 240 sts and 144 sps.

Rnd 17: Ch 3, 2 dc in last ch-2 sp made, ★ † skip next dc, work FPtr around next dc, ch 2, skip next ch-1 sp, sc in next ch-1 sp, (ch 3, sc in next ch-1 sp) 5 times, ch 2, skip next ch-1 sp and next 2 sts, work FPtr around next dc †, (3 dc, ch 2, 3 dc) in next ch-2 sp; repeat from ★ 14 times **more**, then repeat from † to † once, 3 dc in same sp as first dc, hdc in first dc to form last ch-2 sp: 224 sts and 128 sps.

Rnd 18: Ch 3, 8 dc in last ch-2 sp made, ★ † skip next dc, work FPtr around next dc, ch 2, skip next ch-2 sp, sc in next ch-3 sp, (ch 3, sc in next ch-3 sp) 4 times, ch 2, skip next ch-2 sp and next 2 sts, work FPtr around next dc †, 9 dc in next ch-2 sp; repeat from ★ 14 times **more**, then repeat from † to † once; join with slip st to first dc: 256 sts and 96 sps.

Rnd 19: Ch 4 **(counts as first dc plus ch 1, now and throughout)**, dc in next dc, (ch 1, dc in next dc) 7 times, ★ † work FPtr around next FPtr, ch 2, skip next ch-2 sp, sc in next ch-3 sp, (ch 3, sc in next ch-3 sp) 3 times, ch 2, skip next ch-2 sp, work FPtr around next FPtr †, dc in next dc, (ch 1, dc in next dc) 8 times; repeat from ★ 14 times **more**, then repeat from † to † once; join with slip st to first dc: 240 sts and 208 sps.

Rnd 20: (Slip st, ch 1, sc) in first ch-1 sp, ★ † (ch 3, sc in next ch-1 sp) 7 times, skip next dc, work FPdc around next FPtr, ch 2, skip next ch-2 sp, sc in next ch-3 sp, (ch 3, sc in next ch-3 sp) twice, ch 2, skip next ch-2 sp, work FPdc around next FPtr †, sc in next ch-1 sp; repeat from ★ 14 times **more**, then repeat from † to † once; join with slip st to first sc: 208 sts and 176 sps.

Rnd 21: (Slip st, ch 1, sc) in first ch-3 sp, ★ † (ch 3, sc in next ch-3 sp) 6 times, ch 1, skip next sc, work FPtr around next FPdc, ch 2, skip next ch-2 sp, sc in next ch-3 sp, ch 3, sc in next ch-3 sp, ch 2, skip next ch-2 sp, work FPtr around next FPdc, ch 1 †, sc in next ch-3 sp; repeat from ★ 14 times **more**, then repeat from † to † once; join with slip st to first sc: 176 sts and 176 sps.

Rnd 22: (Slip st, ch 1, sc) in first ch-3 sp, ★ † (ch 3, sc in next ch-3 sp) 5 times, ch 1, skip next ch-1 sp, work FPdc around next FPtr, ch 1, skip next ch-2 sp, (dc, ch 3, dc) in next ch-3 sp, ch 1, skip next ch-2 sp, work FPdc around next FPtr, ch 1, skip next ch-1 sp †, sc in next ch-3 sp; repeat from ★ 14 times **more**, then repeat from † to † once; join with slip st to first sc: 160 sts and 160 sps.

Instructions continued on page 23.

Rnd 23: (Slip st, ch 1, sc) in first ch-3 sp, ★ † (ch 3, sc in next ch-3 sp) 4 times, ch 1, skip next ch-1 sp, work FPtr around next FPdc, ch 2, skip next ch-1 sp, (3 dc, ch 3, 3 dc) in next ch-3 sp, ch 2, skip next ch-1 sp, work FPtr around next FPdc, ch 1, skip next ch-1 sp †, sc in next ch-3 sp; repeat from ★ 14 times **more**, then repeat from † to † once; join with slip st to first sc: 208 sts and 144 sps.

Rnd 24: (Slip st, ch 1, sc) in first ch-3 sp, ★ † (ch 3, sc in next ch-3 sp) 3 times, ch 1, skip next ch-1 sp, work FPdc around next FPtr, ch 2, skip next dc, work FPtr around next dc, 3 dc in next ch-3 sp, (ch 2, 3 dc in same sp) twice, skip next dc, work FPtr around next dc, ch 2, skip next ch-2 sp, work FPdc around next FPtr, ch 1, skip next ch-1 sp †, sc in next ch-3 sp; repeat from ★ 14 times **more**, then repeat from † to † once; join with slip st to first sc: 272 sts and 144 sps.

Rnd 25: (Slip st, ch 1, sc) in first ch-3 sp, ★ † (ch 3, sc in next ch-3 sp) twice, ch 1, skip next ch-1 sp, work FPdc around next FPdc, ch 2, skip next ch-2 sp and next 2 sts, work FPtr around next dc, (3 dc, ch 2, 3 dc) in next ch-2 sp, skip next dc, (dc, ch 2, dc) in next dc, (3 dc, ch 2, 3 dc) in next ch-2 sp, skip next dc, work FPtr around next dc, ch 2, skip next ch-2 sp, work FPdc around next FPdc, ch 1, skip next ch-1 sp †, sc in next ch-3 sp; repeat from ★ 14 times **more**, then repeat from † to † once; join with slip st to first sc: 336 sts and 144 sps.

Rnd 26: (Slip st, ch 1, sc) in first ch-3 sp, ★ † ch 3, sc in next ch-3 sp, ch 1, skip next ch-1 sp, work FPtr around next FPdc, ch 1, skip next ch-2 sp and next 2 sts, work FPtr around next dc, (3 dc, ch 2, 3 dc) in next ch-2 sp, [ch 1, (3 dc, ch 2, 3 dc) in next ch-2 sp] twice, skip next dc, work FPtr around next dc, ch 2, skip next ch-2 sp, work FPtr around next FPdc, ch 1, skip next ch-1 sp †, sc in next ch-3 sp; repeat from ★ 14 times **more**, then repeat from † to † once; join with slip st to first sc: 384 sts and 160 sps.

Rnd 27: (Slip st, ch 1, sc) in first ch-3 sp, ★ † ch 1, skip next ch-1 sp, work FPdc around next FPtr, ch 1, skip next ch-1 sp and next 2 sts, work FPtr around next dc, (3 dc, ch 2, 3 dc) in next ch-2 sp, skip next dc, [work First Leg of Split FPtr around next dc, skip next 2 dc, work Second Leg around next dc, (3 dc, ch 2, 3 dc) in next ch-2 sp, skip next dc] twice, work FPtr around next dc, ch 1, skip next ch-2 sp, work FPdc around next FPtr, ch 1, skip next ch-1 sp †, sc in next ch-3 sp; repeat from ★ 14 times **more**, then repeat from † to † once; join with slip st to first sc: 400 sts and 112 sps.

Rnd 28: Slip st in next 7 sts and in next ch-2 sp, ch 4, [dc, (ch 1, dc) 4 times] in same sp, ★ † skip next dc, [work First Leg of Split FPtr around next dc, skip next 3 sts, work Second Leg around next dc, dc in next ch-2 sp, (ch 1, dc in same sp) 5 times, skip next dc] twice, work FPtr around next dc, skip next 2 sts and next ch-1 sp, work First Leg of Split FPtr around next FPdc, skip next sc, work Second Leg around next FPdc, skip next ch and next 2 sts, work FPtr around next dc †, dc in next ch-2 sp, (ch 1, dc in same sp) 5 times; repeat from ★ 14 times **more**, then repeat from † to † once; join with slip st to first dc: 368 sts and 240 sps.

Rnd 29: Ch 1, sc in same st, ★ † (sc in next ch-1 sp and in next dc) twice, (sc, ch 3, sc) in next ch-1 sp, sc in next dc, (sc in next ch-1 sp and in next dc) twice, [(sc, ch 3, sc) in next Split FPtr, sc in next dc, (sc in next ch-1 sp and in next dc) twice, (sc, ch 3, sc) in next ch-1 sp, sc in next dc, (sc in next ch-1 sp and in next dc) twice] 2 times, skip next FPtr, (sc, ch 3, sc) in next Split FPtr, skip next FPtr †, sc in next dc; repeat from ★ 14 times **more**, then repeat from † to † once; join with slip st to first sc, finish off.

See Washing and Blocking, page 2.

Exciting

EXPERIENCED

Finished Size: 12¾" (32.5 cm) diameter

MATERIALS

Bedspread Weight Cotton Thread (size 10) [350 yards (320 meters) per ball]: One ball

Steel crochet hook, size 7 (1.65 mm) **or** size needed for gauge

GAUGE SWATCH: 2¾" (7 cm) diameter

Work same as Doily through Rnd 6.

Stitch Guide

FRONT POST TREBLE CROCHET ***(abbreviated FPtr)***

YO twice, insert hook from **front** to **back** around post of st indicated ***(Fig. 2, page 1)***, YO and pull up a loop (4 loops on hook), (YO and draw through 2 loops on hook) 3 times.

DOILY

Ch 6; join with slip st to form a ring.

Rnd 1 (Right side)**:** Ch 5 **(counts as first dc plus ch 2)**, (2 dc in ring, ch 2) 7 times, dc in ring; join with slip st to first dc: 16 dc and 8 ch-2 sps.

Rnd 2: Slip st in first ch-2 sp, ch 3 **(counts as first dc, now and throughout)**, 2 dc in same sp, work FPtr around next dc, ch 1, ★ 3 dc in next ch-2 sp, work FPtr around next dc, ch 1; repeat from ★ around; join with slip st to first dc: 32 sts and 8 chs.

Instructions continued on page 27.

Rnd 3: Ch 3, dc in next 3 sts, work FPtr around same FPtr, ch 1, skip next ch, ★ dc in next 4 sts, work FPtr around same FPtr, ch 1, skip next ch; repeat from ★ around; join with slip st to first dc: 40 sts and 8 chs.

Rnd 4: Ch 3, dc in next 3 dc, 2 dc in next FPtr, work FPtr around same FPtr, ch 1, skip next ch, ★ dc in next 4 dc, 2 dc in next FPtr, work FPtr around same FPtr, ch 1, skip next ch; repeat from ★ around; join with slip st to first dc: 56 sts and 8 chs.

Rnd 5: Ch 3, dc in next 5 dc, 2 dc in next FPtr, work FPtr around same FPtr, ch 1, skip next ch, ★ dc in next 6 dc, 2 dc in next FPtr, work FPtr around same FPtr, ch 1, skip next ch; repeat from ★ around; join with slip st to first dc: 72 sts and 8 chs.

Rnd 6: Ch 3, dc in next 8 sts, work FPtr around same FPtr, ch 1, skip next ch, ★ dc in next 9 sts, work FPtr around same FPtr, ch 1, skip next ch; repeat from ★ around; join with slip st to first dc: 80 sts and 8 ch-1 sps.

Rnd 7: Ch 3, dc in next 9 sts, work FPtr around same FPtr, ★ dc in next ch-1 sp and in next 10 sts, work FPtr around same FPtr; repeat from ★ around to last ch-1 sp, dc in last ch-1 sp; join with slip st to first dc: 96 sts.

Rnd 8: (Slip st, ch 1, sc) in next dc, ch 3, skip next dc, ★ sc in next dc, ch 3, skip next st; repeat from ★ around; join with slip st to first sc: 48 ch-3 sps.

Rnd 9: (Slip st, ch 1, sc) in first ch-3 sp, (ch 4, sc in next ch-3 sp) around, ch 1, dc in first sc to form last ch-4 sp.

Rnd 10: Ch 1, (sc, ch 3, sc) in last ch-4 sp made, ch 1, ★ (sc, ch 3, sc) in next ch-4 sp, ch 1; repeat from ★ around; join with slip st to first sc: 96 sps.

Rnd 11: Ch 1, **turn**; sc in first ch-1 sp, ★ ch 5, skip next ch-3 sp, sc in next ch-1 sp; repeat from ★ around to last ch-3 sp, ch 4, skip last ch-3 sp, sc in first sc to form last ch-5 sp: 48 ch-5 sps.

Rnd 12: Ch 1, turn; (sc, ch 3, sc) in last ch-5 sp made, ch 2, ★ (sc, ch 3, sc) in next ch-5 sp, ch 2; repeat from ★ around; join with slip st to first sc: 96 sps.

Rnd 13: Ch 1, turn; sc in first ch-2 sp, ch 5, skip next ch-3 sp, sc in next ch-2 sp, ★ ch 5, skip next ch-3 sp, sc in next ch-2 sp; repeat from ★ around to last ch-3 sp, ch 4, skip last ch-3 sp, sc in first sc to form last ch-5 sp: 48 ch-5 sps.

Rnd 14: Ch 1, turn; (sc, ch 3, sc) in last ch-5 sp made, (ch 3, sc) twice in each ch-5 sp around, ch 1, hdc in first sc to form last ch-3 sp: 96 ch-3 sps.

Rnd 15: Ch 1, do **not** turn; sc in last ch-3 sp made, ch 6, skip next ch-3 sp, ★ sc in next ch-3 sp, ch 6, skip next ch-3 sp; repeat from ★ around; join with slip st to first sc: 48 ch-6 sps.

Rnd 16: (Slip st, ch 3, 6 dc) in first ch-6 sp, (sc, ch 3, sc) in next ch-6 sp, ★ 7 dc in next ch-6 sp, (sc, ch 3, sc) in next ch-6 sp; repeat from ★ around; join with slip st to first dc: 216 sts and 24 ch-3 sps.

Rnd 17: Ch 4 **(counts as first dc plus ch 1)**, dc in next dc, (ch 1, dc in next dc) 5 times, skip next ch-3 sp and next sc, ★ dc in next dc, (ch 1, dc in next dc) 6 times, skip next ch-3 sp and next sc; repeat from ★ around; join with slip st to first dc: 144 ch-1 sps.

Rnd 18: (Slip st, ch 1, sc) in first ch-1 sp, (ch 3, sc in next ch-1 sp) 5 times, ch 1, ★ sc in next ch-1 sp, (ch 3, sc in next ch-1 sp) 5 times, ch 1; repeat from ★ around; join with slip st to first sc.

Rnd 19: (Slip st, ch 1, sc) in first ch-3 sp, (ch 3, sc in next ch-3 sp) 4 times, (sc, ch 3, sc) in next ch-1 sp, ★ sc in next ch-3 sp, (ch 3, sc in next ch-3 sp) 4 times, (sc, ch 3, sc) in next ch-1 sp; repeat from ★ around; join with slip st to first sc: 120 ch-3 sps.

Rnd 20: (Slip st, ch 1, sc) in first ch-3 sp, (ch 3, sc in next ch-3 sp) 3 times, ch 5, skip next ch-3 sp, ★ sc in next ch-3 sp, (ch 3, sc in next ch-3 sp) 3 times, ch 5, skip next ch-3 sp; repeat from ★ around; join with slip st to first sc: 96 sps.

Rnd 21: (Slip st, ch 1, sc) in first ch-3 sp, (ch 3, sc in next ch-3 sp) twice, ch 2, (sc, ch 3, sc) in center ch of next ch-5, ch 2, ★ sc in next ch-3 sp, (ch 3, sc in next ch-3 sp) twice, ch 2, (sc, ch 3, sc) in center ch of next ch-5, ch 2; repeat from ★ around; join with slip st to first sc: 120 sps.

Rnd 22: (Slip st, ch 1, sc) in first ch-3 sp, ch 3, sc in next ch-3 sp, ch 9, skip next 3 sps, ★ sc in next ch-3 sp, ch 3, sc in next ch-3 sp, ch 9, skip next 3 sps; repeat from ★ around; join with slip st to first sc: 48 sps.

Rnd 23: (Slip st, ch 1, sc) in first ch-3 sp, 13 dc in next ch-9 sp, (sc in next ch-3 sp, 13 dc in next ch-9 sp) around; join with slip st to first sc: 336 sts.

Rnd 24: (Slip st, ch 1, sc) in next dc, (ch 2, skip next dc, sc in next dc) 6 times, skip next sc, ★ sc in next dc, (ch 2, skip next dc, sc in next dc) 6 times, skip next sc; repeat from ★ around; join with slip st to first sc: 144 ch-2 sps.

Rnd 25: (Slip st, ch 1, sc) in first ch-2 sp, ch 3, (sc in next ch-2 sp, ch 3) 4 times, ★ sc in next 2 ch-2 sps, ch 3, (sc in next ch-2 sp, ch 3) 4 times; repeat from ★ around to last ch-2 sp, sc in last ch-2 sp; join with slip st to first sc: 120 ch-3 sps.

Rnd 26: (Slip st, ch 1, sc, ch 3, sc) in first ch-3 sp, ch 1, ★ (sc, ch 3, sc) in next ch-3 sp, ch 1; repeat from ★ around; join with slip st to first sc: 240 sps.

Rnd 27: Ch 1, **turn**; sc in first ch-1 sp, ★ ch 5, skip next ch-3 sp, sc in next ch-1 sp; repeat from ★ around to last ch-3 sp, ch 4, skip last ch-3 sp, sc in first sc to form last ch-5 sp: 120 ch-5 sps.

Rnd 28: Ch 1, turn; (sc, ch 3, sc) in last ch-5 sp made, ch 1, ★ (sc, ch 3, sc) in next ch-5 sp, ch 1; repeat from ★ around; join with slip st to first sc: 240 sps.

Rnd 29: Ch 1, turn; sc in first ch-1 sp, ★ ch 5, skip next ch-3 sp, sc in next ch-1 sp; repeat from ★ around to last ch-3 sp, ch 4, skip last ch-3 sp, sc in first sc to form last ch-5 sp: 120 ch-5 sps.

Rnd 30: Ch 1, turn; (sc, ch 3, sc) in last ch-5 sp made, ★ ch 2, (sc, ch 3, sc) in next ch-5 sp; repeat from ★ around, hdc in first sc to form last ch-2 sp: 240 sps.

Rnd 31: Ch 1, do **not** turn; (sc, ch 3, sc) in last ch-2 sp made, ★ † (ch 3, skip next ch-3 sp, sc in next ch-2 sp) twice, ch 5, skip next ch-3 sp, (sc in next ch-2 sp, ch 3, skip next ch-3 sp) twice †, (sc, ch 3, sc) in next ch-2 sp; repeat from ★ 22 times **more**, then repeat from † to † once; join with slip st to first sc: 144 sps.

Rnd 32: (Slip st, ch 1, sc, ch 3, sc) in first ch-3 sp, ch 1, (sc, ch 3, sc) in next ch-3 sp, sc in next ch-3 sp, 7 dc in next ch-5 sp, sc in next ch-3 sp, (sc, ch 3, sc) in next ch-3 sp, ★ [ch 1, (sc, ch 3, sc) in next ch-3 sp] twice, sc in next ch-3 sp, 7 dc in next ch-5 sp, sc in next ch-3 sp, (sc, ch 3, sc) in next ch-3 sp; repeat from ★ around, ch 1; join with slip st to first sc, finish off.

See Washing and Blocking, page 2.

Exclusive

EXPERIENCED

Finished Size: 11³/₄" (30 cm) diameter

MATERIALS

Bedspread Weight Cotton Thread (size 10) [350 yards (320 meters) per ball]: One ball

Steel crochet hook, size 7 (1.65 mm) **or** size needed for gauge

GAUGE SWATCH: 2³/₄" (7 cm) diameter.
Work same as Doily, page 31, through Rnd 6.

Stitch Guide

DOUBLE TREBLE CROCHET ***(abbreviated dtr)***
YO 3 times, insert hook in dc indicated, YO and pull up a loop (5 loops on hook), (YO and draw through 2 loops on hook) 4 times.

BACK POST SINGLE CROCHET ***(abbreviated BPsc)***
Insert hook from **back** to **front** around post of dc indicated ***(Fig. 2, page 1)***, YO and pull up a loop, YO and draw through both loops on hook.

FRONT POST SINGLE CROCHET ***(abbreviated FPsc)***
Insert hook from **front** to **back** around post of st indicated ***(Fig. 2, page 1)***, YO and pull up a loop, YO and draw through both loops on hook.

FRONT POST TREBLE CROCHET ***(abbreviated FPtr)***
YO twice, insert hook from **front** to **back** around post of st indicated ***(Fig. 2, page 1)***, YO and pull up a loop (4 loops on hook), (YO and draw through 2 loops on hook) 3 times.

SPLIT DC (uses 2 ch-3 sps)
First Leg: YO, insert hook in same ch-3 sp as last dc made, YO and pull up a loop, YO and draw through 2 loops on hook (2 loops remaining on hook).
Second Leg: YO, insert hook in ch-3 sp indicated, YO and pull up a loop, YO and draw through 2 loops on hook, YO and draw through all 3 loops on hook.

SPLIT CLUSTER (uses next 7 sts)
YO twicc, † inscrt hook from **front** to **back** around post of **next** FPtr ***(Fig. 2, page 1)***, YO and pull up a loop, (YO and draw through 2 loops on hook) twice †, YO, skip next 2 dc, insert hook in next Split dc, YO and pull up a loop, YO and draw through 2 loops on hook, YO twice, skip next 2 dc, repeat from † to † once, YO and draw through all 4 loops on hook.

SC DECREASE
Pull up a loop in next 2 ch-3 sps, YO and draw through all 3 loops on hook.

Instructions continued on page 31.

DOILY

Ch 6; join with slip st to form a ring.

Rnd 1 (Right side)**:** Ch 3 **(counts as first dc, now and throughout)**, 11 dc in ring; join with slip st to first dc: 12 dc.

Rnd 2: Ch 3, dc in same st, (ch 2, 2 dc in next dc) around, ch 1, sc in first dc to form last ch-2 sp: 24 dc and 12 ch-2 sps.

Rnd 3: Ch 3, 2 dc in last ch-2 sp made, 5 dc in each ch-2 sp around, 2 dc in same sp as first dc; join with slip st to first dc: 60 dc.

Rnd 4: Ch 1, sc in same st, ★ ch 5, skip next 4 dc, sc in next dc; repeat from ★ around to last 4 dc, ch 2, skip last 4 dc, dc in first sc to form last ch-5 sp: 12 sc and 12 ch-5 sps.

Rnd 5: Ch 3, 3 dc in last ch-5 sp made, work FPtr around next sc, (7 dc in next ch-5 sp, work FPtr around next sc) around, 3 dc in same sp as first dc; join with slip st to first dc: 96 sts.

Rnd 6: Ch 1, sc in same st and in next 3 dc, work FPsc around next FPtr, (sc in next 7 dc, work FPsc around next FPtr) around to last 3 dc, sc in last 3 dc; join with slip st to first sc.

Rnd 7: Ch 1, working **behind** Rnd 6, work BPsc around first dc on Rnd 5, ch 7, (work BPsc around center dc of next 7-dc group on Rnd 5, ch 7) around; join with slip st to first BPsc: 12 BPsc and 12 ch-7 sps.

Rnd 8: (Slip st, ch 3, 8 dc) in first ch-7 sp, work FPtr around next BPsc, (9 dc in next ch-7 sp, work FPtr around next BPsc) around; join with slip st to first dc: 120 sts.

Rnd 9: Ch 1, sc in same st and in next 8 dc, work FPsc around next FPtr, (sc in next 9 dc, work FPsc around next FPtr) around; join with slip st to Back Loop Only of first sc ***(Fig. 1, page 1)***.

Rnd 10: Working in Back Loops Only, (slip st, ch 1, sc) in next sc, (ch 3, skip next sc, sc in next sc) 3 times, ★ (skip next sc, sc in next st) twice, (ch 3, skip next sc, sc in next sc) 3 times; repeat from ★ around to last 3 sts, skip next sc, sc in next FPsc, skip last st; join with slip st to **both** loops of first sc: 60 sc and 36 ch-3 sps.

Rnd 11: (Slip st, ch 1, sc) in first ch-3 sp, (ch 3, sc in next ch-3 sp) twice, skip next sc, 5 dc in both loops of next sc, ★ sc in next ch-3 sp, (ch 3, sc in next ch-3 sp) twice, skip next sc, 5 dc in both loops of next sc; repeat from ★ around; join with slip st to both loops of first sc: 96 sts and 24 ch-3 sps.

Rnd 12: (Slip st, ch 1, sc) in first ch-3 sp, ★ † ch 3, sc in next ch-3 sp, skip next sc, working in Back Loops Only, 2 dc in next dc, dc in next dc, 3 dc in next dc, dc in next dc, 2 dc in next dc †, sc in next ch-3 sp; repeat from ★ 10 times **more**, then repeat from † to † once; join with slip st to **both** loops of first sc: 132 sts and 12 ch-3 sps.

Rnd 13: (Slip st, ch 1, sc) in first ch-3 sp, working in both loops, ★ † skip next sc, dc in next dc, working in **front** of Rnd 12 and in free loops of dc on Rnd 11 ***(Fig. 4)***, dtr in first dc of 5-dc group, dc in next dc on Rnd 12, dtr in next dc on Rnd 11, dc in next 2 dc on Rnd 12, dtr in next dc on Rnd 11, dc in same st on Rnd 12 as last dc made and in next dc, (dtr in same dc on Rnd 11 as last dtr made, dc in same st on Rnd 12 as last dc made and in next dc) twice, (dtr in next dc on Rnd 11, dc in next dc on Rnd 12) twice †, sc in next ch-3 sp; repeat from ★ 10 times **more**, then repeat from † to † once; join with slip st to first sc: 240 sts.

Fig. 4

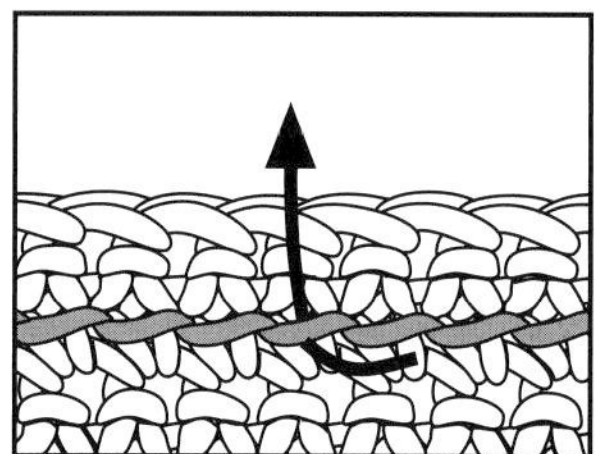

Rnd 14: Ch 1, (work FPsc around next dtr, ch 3) 6 times, ★ work FPsc around each of next 2 dtr, ch 3, (work FPsc around next dtr, ch 3) 5 times; repeat from ★ around to last dtr, work FPsc around last dtr; join with slip st to first FPsc.

Rnd 15: Ch 1, working **behind** Rnd 14 and in sts on Rnd 13, sc in first dc, (ch 3, skip next 2 sts, sc in next st) 6 times, skip next sc, ★ sc in next dc, (ch 3, skip next 2 sts, sc in next st) 6 times, skip next sc; repeat from ★ around; join with slip st to first sc: 84 sc and 72 ch-3 sps.

Rnd 16: (Slip st, ch 2, 2 dc) in first ch-3 sp, ★ † work FPtr around next sc, (3 dc in next ch-3 sp, work FPtr around next sc) 4 times, 2 dc in next ch-3 sp †, work Split dc working First Leg in same sp as last dc made and Second Leg in next ch-3 sp, 2 dc in same sp as Second Leg of last Split dc made; repeat from ★ 10 times **more**, then repeat from † to † once, work Split dc working First Leg in same sp as last dc made and Second Leg in same sp as first dc; skip beginning ch-2 and join with slip st to first dc: 264 sts.

Rnd 17: Slip st in next 3 sts, ch 3, dc in next 2 dc, (work FPtr around next FPtr, dc in next 3 dc) 3 times, work Split Cluster, ★ dc in next 3 dc, (work FPtr around next FPtr, dc in next 3 dc) 3 times, work Split Cluster; repeat from ★ around; join with slip st to first dc: 192 sts.

Rnd 18: Ch 1, sc in same st and in next 2 dc, work FPsc around next FPtr, (sc in next 3 dc, work FPsc around next FPtr) twice, ★ sc in next 7 sts, work FPsc around next FPtr, (sc in next 3 dc, work FPsc around next FPtr) twice; repeat from ★ around to last 4 sts, sc in last 4 sts; join with slip st to Back Loop Only of first sc.

Rnd 19: Ch 1, working in Back Loops Only, sc in same st, (ch 3, skip next st, sc in next sc) 3 times, ch 1, ★ skip next st, sc in next sc, (ch 3, skip next st, sc in next sc) 3 times, ch 1; repeat from ★ around; join with slip st to **both** loops of first sc: 96 sc and 96 sps.

Rnd 20: (Slip st, ch 1, sc) in first ch-3 sp, (ch 3, sc in next ch-3 sp) twice, 5 dc in next ch-1 sp, ★ sc in next ch-3 sp, (ch 3, sc in next ch-3 sp) twice, 5 dc in next ch-1 sp; repeat from ★ around; join with slip st to first sc: 192 sts and 48 ch-3 sps.

Rnd 21: (Slip st, ch 1, sc) in first ch-3 sp, ★ † ch 3, sc in next ch-3 sp, skip next sc, working in Back Loops Only, 2 dc in next dc, dc in next dc, 3 dc in next dc, dc in next dc, 2 dc in next dc †, sc in next ch-3 sp; repeat from ★ 22 times **more**, then repeat from † to † once; join with slip st to **both** loops of first sc: 264 sts and 24 ch-3 sps.

Rnd 22: (Slip st, ch 1, sc) in first ch-3 sp, working in both loops ★ † skip next sc, dc in next dc, working in **front** of Rnd 21 and in free loops of dc on Rnd 20, dtr in first dc of 5-dc group, dc in next dc on Rnd 21, dtr in next dc on Rnd 20, dc in next 2 dc on Rnd 21, dtr in next dc on Rnd 20, dc in same st on Rnd 21 as last dc made and in next dc, (dtr in same dc on Rnd 20 as last dtr made, dc in same st on Rnd 21 as last dc made and in next dc) twice, (dtr in next dc on Rnd 20, dc in next dc on Rnd 21) twice †, sc in next ch-3 sp; repeat from ★ 22 times **more**, then repeat from † to † once; join with slip st to first sc: 480 sts.

Rnd 23: Ch 1, (work FPsc around next dtr, ch 3) 6 times, ★ work FPsc around each of next 2 dtr, ch 3, (work FPsc around next dtr, ch 3) 5 times; repeat from ★ around to last dtr, work FPsc around last dtr; join with slip st to first FPsc.

Rnd 24: Ch 1, working **behind** Rnd 23 and in sts on Rnd 22, sc in first dc, (ch 3, skip next 2 sts, sc in next st) 6 times, skip next sc, ★ sc in next dc, (ch 3, skip next 2 sts, sc in next st) 6 times, skip next sc; repeat from ★ around; join with slip st to first sc: 144 ch-3 sps.

Rnd 25: (Slip st, ch 1, sc) in first ch-3 sp, ch 3, (sc in next ch-3 sp, ch 3) 4 times, ★ sc decrease, ch 3, (sc in next ch-3 sp, ch 3) 4 times; repeat from ★ around to last ch-3 sp, pull up a loop in last ch-3 sp, insert hook in first sc, YO and pull up a loop, YO and draw through all 3 loops on hook to complete last sc decrease: 120 sts and 120 ch-3 sps.

Rnd 26: (Slip st, ch 1, sc) in first ch-3 sp, (ch 3, sc in next ch-3 sp) 4 times, dc in next sc decrease, ★ sc in next ch-3 sp, (ch 3, sc in next ch-3 sp) 4 times, dc in next sc decrease; repeat from ★ around; join with slip st to first sc: 144 sts and 96 ch-3 sps.

Instructions continued on page 37.

Extravagant

Shown on Back Cover.

Stitch Guide

BACK POST SINGLE CROCHET ***(abbreviated BPsc)***
Insert hook from **back** to **front** around post of st indicated ***(Fig. 2, page 1)***, YO and pull up a loop, YO and draw through both loops on hook.

BACK POST HALF DOUBLE CROCHET ***(abbreviated BPhdc)***
YO, insert hook from **back** to **front** around post of st indicated ***(Fig. 2, page 1)***, YO and pull up a loop, YO and draw through all 3 loops on hook.

FRONT POST DOUBLE CROCHET ***(abbreviated FPdc)***
YO, insert hook from **front** to **back** around post of st indicated ***(Fig. 2, page 1)***, YO and pull up a loop (3 loops on hook), (YO and draw through 2 loops on hook) twice.

FRONT POST TREBLE CROCHET ***(abbreviated FPtr)***
YO twice, insert hook from **front** to **back** around post of st indicated ***(Fig. 2, page 1)***, YO and pull up a loop (4 loops on hook), (YO and draw through 2 loops on hook) 3 times.

BACK POST TREBLE CROCHET ***(abbreviated BPtr)***
YO twice, insert hook from **back** to **front** around post of st indicated ***(Fig. 2, page 1)***, YO and pull up a loop (4 loops on hook), (YO and draw through 2 loops on hook) 3 times. Skip st in front of BPtr.

SPLIT FRONT POST DOUBLE CROCHET ***(abbreviated Split FPdc)***
YO, † insert hook from **front** to **back** around post of **next** BPtr ***(Fig. 2, page 1)***, YO and pull up a loop, YO and draw through 2 loops on hook †, YO, skip next sc, repeat from † to † once, YO and draw through all 3 loops on hook.

SPLIT FRONT POST TREBLE CROCHET ***(abbreviated Split FPtr)***

First Leg: YO twice, insert hook from **front** to **back** around post of st indicated ***(Fig. 2, page 1)***, YO and pull up a loop, (YO and draw through 2 loops on hook) twice (2 loops remaining on hook).

Second Leg: YO twice, insert hook from **front** to **back** around post of st indicated, YO and pull up a loop, (YO and draw through 2 loops on hook) twice, YO and draw through all 3 loops on hook.

FRONT POST CLUSTER ***(abbreviated FP Cluster)***
(uses 2 FPtr and one ch-3 sp)
YO twice, † insert hook from **front** to **back** around post of next FPtr ***(Fig. 2, page 1)***, YO and pull up a loop, (YO and draw through 2 loops on hook) twice †, YO, insert hook in next ch-3 sp, YO and pull up a loop, YO and draw through 2 loops on hook, YO twice, skip next sc, repeat from † to † once, YO and draw through all 4 loops on hook.

CLUSTER (uses next 3 sts)
† YO, insert hook in **next** dc, YO and pull up a loop, YO and draw through 2 loops on hook †, YO twice, insert hook from **front** to **back** around post of next FPtr ***(Fig. 2, page 1)***, YO and pull up a loop (5 loops on hook), (YO and draw through 2 loops on hook) twice, repeat from † to † once, YO and draw through all 4 loops on hook.

DECREASE (uses next 5 sts)
YO twice, insert hook from **front** to **back** around post of next FPtr ***(Fig. 2, page 1)***, YO and pull up a loop, (YO and draw through 2 loops on hook) twice, ★ YO twice, skip **next** dc, insert hook from **front** to **back** around post of **next** st, YO and pull up a loop, (YO and draw through 2 loops on hook) twice; repeat from ★ once **more**, YO and draw through all 4 loops on hook.

DC DECREASE (uses next 3 sc)
★ YO, insert hook in Back Loop Only of **next** sc, YO and pull up a loop, YO and draw through 2 loops on hook; repeat from ★ 2 times **more**, YO and draw through all 4 loops on hook.

DOILY

Ch 6; join with slip st to form a ring.

Rnd 1 (Right side): Ch 5 **(counts as first dc plus ch 2)**, dc in ring, (ch 2, dc in ring) 10 times, hdc in first dc to form last ch-2 sp: 12 dc and 12 ch-2 sps.

Rnd 2: Ch 3 **(counts as first dc, now and throughout)**, dc in last ch-2 sp made, work FPtr around next dc, (3 dc in next ch-2 sp, work FPtr around next dc) around, dc in same sp as first dc; join with slip st to first dc: 48 sts.

Rnd 3: Ch 3, (dc, ch 2, 2 dc) in same st, skip next dc, work FPtr around next FPtr, skip next dc, ★ (2 dc, ch 2, 2 dc) in next dc, skip next dc, work FPtr around next FPtr, skip next dc; repeat from ★ around; join with slip st to first dc: 60 sts and 12 ch-2 sps.

Rnd 4: Slip st in next dc and in next ch-2 sp, ch 3, 4 dc in same sp, ★ † ch 1, work First Leg of Split FPtr around next dc, skip next 3 sts, work Second Leg around next dc, ch 1 †, 5 dc in next ch-2 sp; repeat from ★ 10 times **more**, then repeat from † to † once; join with slip st to first dc: 72 sts and 24 ch-1 sps.

Rnd 5: Ch 3, ★ † work FPtr around next dc, (2 dc, ch 2, 2 dc) in next dc, work FPtr around next dc, dc in next dc, working **behind** next Split FPtr, work BPtr around skipped FPtr on Rnd 3 †, dc in next dc on Rnd 4; repeat from ★ 10 times **more**, then repeat from † to † once; join with slip st to first dc: 108 sts and 12 ch-2 sps.

Rnd 6: Slip st in next 3 sts and in next ch-2 sp, ch 3, (2 dc, ch 3, 3 dc) in same sp, ch 1, skip next 2 dc, decrease, ch 1, ★ (3 dc, ch 3, 3 dc) in next ch-2 sp, ch 1, skip next 2 dc, decrease, ch 1; repeat from ★ around; join with slip st to first dc: 84 sts and 36 sps.

Instructions continued on page 35.

Rnd 7: Slip st in next 2 sts and in next ch-3 sp, ch 3, 6 dc in same sp, ★ † skip next dc, work FPtr around next dc, ch 2, skip next dc, sc in next decrease, ch 2, skip next dc, work FPtr around next dc †, 7 dc in next ch-3 sp; repeat from ★ 10 times **more**, then repeat from † to † once; join with slip st to first dc: 120 sts and 24 ch-2 sps.

Rnd 8: Ch 4 **(counts as first dc plus ch 1, now and throughout)**, dc in Back Loop Only of next dc ***(Fig. 1, page 1)***, (ch 1, dc in Back Loop Only of next dc) 5 times, ★ † work First Leg of Split FPtr around next FPtr, skip next sc, work Second Leg around next FPtr †, dc in Back Loop Only of next dc, (ch 1, dc in Back Loop Only of next dc) 6 times; repeat from ★ 10 times **more**, then repeat from † to † once; join with slip st to first dc: 96 sts and 72 ch-1 sps.

Rnd 9: Ch 1, work BPsc around same st, (ch 3, work BPsc around next dc) 6 times, skip next Split FPtr, ★ work BPsc around next dc, (ch 3, work BPsc around next dc) 6 times, skip next Split FPtr; repeat from ★ around; join with slip st to first BPsc: 72 ch-3 sps.

Rnd 10: (Slip st, ch 1, sc) in first ch-3 sp, (ch 3, sc in next ch-3 sp) 5 times, ch 1, ★ sc in next ch-3 sp, (ch 3, sc in next ch-3 sp) 5 times, ch 1; repeat from ★ around; join with slip st to first sc.

Rnd 11: (Slip st, ch 1, sc) in first ch-3 sp, (ch 3, sc in next ch-3 sp) 4 times, (dc, ch 2, dc) in next ch-1 sp, ★ sc in next ch-3 sp, (ch 3, sc in next ch-3 sp) 4 times, (dc, ch 2, dc) in next ch-1 sp; repeat from ★ around; join with slip st to first sc: 84 sts and 60 sps.

Rnd 12: (Slip st, ch 1, sc) in first ch-3 sp, ★ † (ch 3, sc in next ch-3 sp) 3 times, skip next sc, work FPtr around next dc, (2 dc, ch 2, 2 dc) in next ch-2 sp, work FPtr around next dc †, sc in next ch-3 sp; repeat from ★ 10 times **more**, then repeat from † to † once; join with slip st to first sc: 120 sts and 48 sps.

Rnd 13: (Slip st, ch 1, sc) in first ch-3 sp, ★ † (ch 3, sc in next ch-3 sp) twice, skip next sc, work FPtr around next FPtr, ch 1, (3 dc, ch 3, 3 dc) in next ch-2 sp, ch 1, skip next 2 dc, work FPtr around next FPtr †, sc in next ch-3 sp; repeat from ★ 10 times **more**, then repeat from † to † once; join with slip st to first sc: 132 sts and 60 sps.

Rnd 14: (Slip st, ch 1, sc) in first ch-3 sp, ★ † ch 3, sc in next ch-3 sp, skip next sc, work FPtr around next FPtr, ch 1, dc in next dc, work FPtr around next dc, dc in next dc, (3 dc, ch 3, 3 dc) in next ch-3 sp, dc in next dc, work FPtr around next dc, dc in next dc, ch 1, work FPtr around next FPtr †, sc in next ch-3 sp; repeat from ★ 10 times **more**, then repeat from † to † once; join with slip st to first sc: 192 sts and 48 sps.

Rnd 15: Working in sts and chs, slip st in next 7 sts, ch 3, ★ † work FPtr around next FPtr, dc in next dc, ch 1, skip next dc, work FPtr around next dc, 9 dc in next ch-3 sp, skip next dc, work FPtr around next dc, ch 1, skip next dc, dc in next dc, work FPtr around next FPtr, dc in next dc, ch 1, work FP Cluster, ch 1 †, dc in next dc; repeat from ★ 10 times **more**, then repeat from † to † once; join with slip st to first dc: 216 sts and 48 chs.

Rnd 16: Working in sts and chs, slip st in next 4 sts and in Back Loop Only of next dc, ch 4, dc in Back Loop Only of next dc, (ch 1, dc in Back Loop Only of next dc) 7 times, ★ † work FPtr around next FPtr, work Cluster, (2 dc, ch 2, 2 dc) in next FP Cluster, work Cluster, work FPtr around next FPtr †, dc in Back Loop Only of next dc, (ch 1, dc in Back Loop Only of next dc) 8 times; repeat from ★ 10 times **more**, then repeat from † to † once; join with slip st to first dc: 204 sts and 108 sps.

Rnd 17: Ch 1, work BPsc around same st, ★ † (ch 3, work BPsc around next dc) 8 times, work BPsc around next FPtr, ch 1, work FPtr around center post of next Cluster, (2 dc, ch 2, 2 dc) in next ch-2 sp, skip next 2 dc, work FPtr around center post of next Cluster, ch 1, work BPsc around next FPtr †, work BPsc around next dc; repeat from ★ 10 times **more**, then repeat from † to † once; join with slip st to first BPsc: 204 sts and 132 sps.

Rnd 18: (Slip st, ch 1, sc) in first ch-3 sp, ★ † (ch 3, sc in next ch-3 sp) 7 times, skip next 2 BPsc, work FPtr around each of next 2 sts, 5 dc in next ch-2 sp, skip next dc, work FPtr around each of next 2 sts, skip next ch-1 sp †, sc in next ch-3 sp; repeat from ★ 10 times **more**, then repeat from † to † once; join with slip st to first sc: 204 sts and 84 sps.

Rnd 19: (Slip st, ch 1, sc) in first ch-3 sp, ★ † (ch 3, sc in next ch-3 sp) 6 times, skip next sc, work FPtr around next FPtr, skip next FPtr, sc in next dc, (ch 2, sc in next dc) 4 times, skip next FPtr, work FPtr around next FPtr †, sc in next ch-3 sp; repeat from ★ 10 times **more**, then repeat from † to † once; join with slip st to first sc: 168 sts and 120 sps.

Rnd 20: (Slip st, ch 1, sc) in first ch-3 sp, ★ † (ch 3, sc in next ch-3 sp) 5 times, skip next sc, work FPtr around next FPtr, ch 1, sc in next ch-2 sp, (ch 2, sc in next ch-2 sp) 3 times, ch 1, skip next sc, work FPtr around next FPtr †, sc in next ch-3 sp; repeat from ★ 10 times **more**, then repeat from † to † once; join with slip st to first sc: 144 sts and 120 sps.

Rnd 21: (Slip st, ch 1, sc) in first ch-3 sp, ★ † (ch 3, sc in next ch-3 sp) 4 times, skip next sc, work FPtr around next FPtr, ch 3, skip next ch-1 sp, sc in next ch-2 sp, (ch 2, sc in next ch-2 sp) twice, ch 3, skip next ch-1 sp, work FPtr around next FPtr †, sc in next ch-3 sp; repeat from ★ 10 times **more**, then repeat from † to † once; join with slip st to first sc: 120 sts and 96 sps.

Rnd 22: (Slip st, ch 1, sc) in first ch-3 sp, ★ † (ch 3, sc in next ch-3 sp) 3 times, skip next sc, work FPtr around next FPtr, ch 5, skip next ch-3 sp, sc in next ch-2 sp, ch 2, sc in next ch-2 sp, ch 5, skip next ch-3 sp, work FPtr around next FPtr †, sc in next ch-3 sp; repeat from ★ 10 times **more**, then repeat from † to † once; join with slip st to first sc: 96 sts and 72 sps.

Rnd 23: (Slip st, ch 1, sc) in first ch-3 sp, ★ † (ch 3, sc in next ch-3 sp) twice, skip next sc, work FPtr around next FPtr, ch 7, skip next ch-5 sp, 3 sc in next ch-2 sp, ch 7, skip next ch-5 sp, work FPtr around next FPtr †, sc in next ch-3 sp; repeat from ★ 10 times **more**, then repeat from † to † once; join with slip st to first sc: 96 sts and 48 sps.

Rnd 24: (Slip st, ch 1, sc) in first ch-3 sp, ★ † ch 3, sc in next ch-3 sp, skip next sc, work FPtr around next FPtr, ch 9, sc in next ch-7 sp, sc in next 3 sc and in next ch-7 sp, ch 9, work FPtr around next FPtr †, sc in next ch-3 sp; repeat from ★ 10 times **more**, then repeat from † to † once; join with slip st to first sc: 108 sts and 36 sps.

Rnd 25: Slip st in first ch-3 sp, ch 3, ★ † skip next sc, work FPtr around next FPtr, dc in next 4 chs, 3 dc in next ch, dc in next 4 chs, dc in Back Loop Only of next sc, work dc decrease, dc in Back Loop Only of next sc, dc in next 4 chs, 3 dc in next ch, dc in next 4 chs, work FPtr around next FPtr †, dc in next ch-3 sp; repeat from ★ 10 times **more**, then repeat from † to † once; join with slip st to first dc: 336 sts.

Rnd 26: Ch 3, dc in same st, work BPhdc around each of next 13 sts, (3 dc in next st, work BPhdc around each of next 13 sts) around, dc in same st as first dc; join with slip st to first dc: 384 sts.

Rnd 27: Ch 3, dc in same st, ★ † work FPtr around next dc, ch 2, skip next BPhdc, (sc in next BPhdc, ch 2, skip next BPhdc) 6 times, work FPtr around next dc †, 3 dc in next dc; repeat from ★ 22 times **more**, then repeat from † to † once, dc in same st as first dc; join with slip st to first dc: 264 sts and 168 ch-2 sps.

Rnd 28: Ch 3, dc in same st, ★ † work FPtr around next dc, work BPtr around next FPtr, ch 2, skip next ch-2 sp, (sc in next ch-2 sp, ch 2) 5 times, skip next ch-2 sp, work BPtr around next FPtr, work FPtr around next dc †, 3 dc in next dc; repeat from ★ 22 times **more**, then repeat from † to † once, dc in same st as first dc; join with slip st to first dc: 288 sts and 144 ch-2 sps.

Rnd 29: Ch 3, dc in same st, ★ † work FPtr around next dc, work BPtr around each of next 2 sts, ch 2, skip next ch-2 sp, (sc in next ch-2 sp, ch 2) 4 times, skip next ch-2 sp, work BPtr around each of next 2 sts, work FPtr around next dc †, 3 dc in next dc; repeat from ★ 22 times **more**, then repeat from † to † once, dc in same st as first dc; join with slip st to first dc: 312 sts and 120 ch-2 sps.

Rnd 30: Ch 3, dc in same st, ★ † work FPtr around next dc, work BPtr around each of next 3 sts, ch 2, skip next ch-2 sp, (sc in next ch-2 sp, ch 2) 3 times, skip next ch-2 sp, work BPtr around each of next 3 sts, work FPtr around next dc †, 3 dc in next dc; repeat from ★ 22 times **more**, then repeat from † to † once, dc in same st as first dc; join with slip st to first dc: 336 sts and 96 ch-2 sps.

Instructions continued on page 37.

Rnd 31: Ch 3, dc in same st, ★ † work FPtr around next dc, work BPtr around each of next 4 sts, ch 2, skip next ch-2 sp, (sc in next ch-2 sp, ch 2) twice, skip next ch-2 sp, work BPtr around each of next 4 sts, work FPtr around next dc †, 3 dc in next dc; repeat from ★ 22 times **more**, then repeat from † to † once, dc in same st as first dc; join with slip st to first dc: 360 sts and 72 ch-2 sps.

Rnd 32: Ch 3, dc in same st, ★ † work FPtr around next dc, work BPtr around each of next 5 sts, ch 2, skip next ch-2 sp, sc in next ch-2 sp, ch 2, skip next ch-2 sp, work BPtr around each of next 5 sts, work FPtr around next dc †, 3 dc in next dc; repeat from ★ 22 times **more**, then repeat from † to † once, dc in same st as first dc; join with slip st to first dc: 384 sts and 48 ch-2 sps.

Rnd 33: Ch 1, [slip st from **front** to **back** around post of same st, ch 3 **(first FPdc made)**], work FPdc around each of next 6 sts, work Split FPdc, (work FPdc around each of next 13 sts, work Split FPdc) around to last 6 sts, work FPdc around each of last 6 sts; join with slip st to first FPdc: 336 sts.

Rnd 34: Ch 1, sc in same st, ch 3, skip next st, ★ sc in next st, ch 3, skip next st; repeat from ★ around; join with slip st to first sc, finish off.

See Washing and Blocking, page 2.

Exclusive *Continued from page 32.*

Rnd 27: (Slip st, ch 1, sc) in first ch-3 sp, (ch 3, sc in next ch-3 sp) 3 times, skip next sc, 3 dc in next dc, ★ sc in next ch-3 sp, (ch 3, sc in next ch-3 sp) 3 times, skip next sc, 3 dc in next dc; repeat from ★ around; join with slip st to first sc: 168 sts and 72 ch-3 sps.

Rnd 28: (Slip st, ch 1, sc) in first ch-3 sp, ★ † (ch 3, sc in next ch-3 sp) twice, skip next sc, 2 dc in next dc, dc in next dc, 2 dc in next dc †, sc in next ch-3 sp; repeat from ★ 22 times **more**, then repeat from † to † once; join with slip st to first sc: 192 sts and 48 ch-3 sps.

Rnd 29: (Slip st, ch 1, sc) in first ch-3 sp, ★ † ch 3, sc in next ch-3 sp, skip next sc, working in Back Loops Only, 2 dc in next dc, dc in next dc, 3 dc in next dc, dc in next dc, 2 dc in next dc †, sc in next ch-3 sp; repeat from ★ 22 times **more**, then repeat from † to † once; join with slip st to **both** loops of first sc: 264 sts and 24 ch-3 sps.

Rnd 30: (Slip st, ch 1, sc) in first ch-3 sp, working in both loops, ★ † skip next sc, dc in next dc, working in **front** of Rnd 29 and in free loops of dc on Rnd 28, dtr in first dc of 5-dc group, dc in next dc on Rnd 29, dtr in next dc on Rnd 28, dc in next 2 dc on Rnd 29, dtr in next dc on Rnd 28, dc in same st on Rnd 29 as last dc made and in next dc, (dtr in same dc on Rnd 28 as last dtr made, dc in same st on Rnd 29 as last dc made and in next dc) twice, (dtr in next dc on Rnd 28, dc in next dc on Rnd 29) twice †, sc in next ch-3 sp; repeat from ★ 22 times **more**, then repeat from † to † once; join with slip st to first sc: 480 sts.

Rnd 31: Ch 1, (work FPsc around next dtr, ch 3) 6 times, ★ work FPsc around each of next 2 dtr, ch 3, (work FPsc around next dtr, ch 3) 5 times; repeat from ★ around to last dtr, work FPsc around last dtr; join with slip st to first FPsc, finish off.

See Washing and Blocking, page 2.